GUNS AND YELLO⋯

The book is not a flag-waving exercise but a critical look at the Kargil war, which left twelve hundred men — approximately five hundred Indian soldiers and seven hundred Pakistani intruders — dead. Another eleven hundred Indian soldiers were maimed, half of them permanently.

Through ten essays by commentators who either covered the Kargil war or followed it closely, the book takes us to the theatre of war and makes us experience what it was like for the jawans and the young officers fighting there. Instead of turning sentimental or jingoistic, however, the essays bring out the abysmal failures of the Indian intelligence set-up, the army and the government which led to the fiasco. The essays also bring out the feelings of frustration and anger that the jawans and officers felt towards their leadership for thrusting an avoidable war on them and later for not allowing them to cross the Line of Control into Pakistan.

The book attempts to sift through competing versions of perceptions and reality — Indian, Pakistani, Kashmiri and of the international community — to get at the "truth" about Kargil as well as Kashmir, in whose name the war was fought.

GUNS AND YELLOW ROSES

Essays on the Kargil War

HarperCollins *Publishers* India

HarperCollins *Publishers* India Pvt Ltd
7/16 Ansari Road, Daryaganj, New Delhi 110 002

Copyright © HarperCollins *Publishers* India Pvt Ltd 1999

First published in 1999 by
HarperCollins *Publishers* India

ISBN 81-7223-373-6

Credits:
KBK for the Kargil map on page no. 6
Saurabh Das for photographs on page nos. 1, 17, 20, 29, 31, 85, 89, 91, 139, 153, 167, 171, 174, 185, 195, 227
Pamela Constable for photographs on page nos. 35, 47, 48, 49, 51, 52, 56, 63, 95, 151
PANA for photograph on page no. 207

Typeset by
Nikita Overseas Pvt Ltd
19A Ansari Road
New Delhi 110 002

Printed in India by
Gopsons Papers Ltd
A-14 Sector 60
Noida 201 301

All rights reserved. No part of this book may be reproduced, stored in a retrieval system, or transmitted, in any form, or by any means, electronic or mechanical, photocopying, recording or otherwise, without the prior permission of the publishers.

Contents

Acknowledgements	*vii*
Sankarshan Thakur Journeys Without Maps	1
Pamela Constable Selective Truths	35
Muzamil Jaleel 'It Was Not Our War'	63
Bharat Bhushan In the 'Enemy Country'	95
Saurabh Das An Emotional Assignment	123
Rahul Bedi A Dismal Failure	139
Lt. Gen. Moti Dar Blundering Through	167
J.N. Dixit A Defining Moment	185
Sunanda K. Datta-Ray Winning a Reprieve	207
Suketu Mehta A Fatal Love	227
Notes on Contributors	245

ACKNOWLEDGEMENTS

The Publishers are grateful to all the contributors for readily agreeing to write the essays in spite of their hectic schedules. We would like to thank Saurabh Das and Pamela Constable for letting us use their photographs, and Raj Kamal Jha, deputy editor of *The Indian Express*, for his valuable suggestions when the book was being conceptualised.

JOURNEYS WITHOUT MAPS

■ SANKARSHAN THAKUR

> The associate editor of *The Telegraph*, who was in Kargil for six weeks, writes about guns, yellow roses and other highs and lows of covering "a pretty little ugly war."

Journeys Without Maps

For a few weeks midsummer, between the melting of snow and the onset of sleet, Kargil is awash with yellow roses. Kargilis have an odd passion for picking them and sticking them into their mouths. They make a queer-comic sight, like overgrown babies suckling on oversize soothers. But faith turns on its own illogic. Kargilis chew on yellow roses in the belief that it is good for the body and the soul and the future.

This summer there wasn't enough time to pick flowers, though. And eventually there weren't enough people to pick them. War had brought a desperate season to Kargil. The yellow roses stood mostly unclaimed. Military convoys moved up and down and the dust from their tyres and gunpowder from the artillery settled on them. The rain would oft come and wash them and restore their freshness but the trucks and the guns this summer were quite unrelenting.

When I had first gone to Kargil in the September of 1998 in search of a story to tell, it didn't look remotely like a place roses could bloom in. The mountains were bare but for moss which had caught the chill and turned an unreal mauve. The snows were about to fall and Zojila Pass about to close for the winter. Kargil was already preparing for its long hibernation — its high mountains aloof and its valleys stripped to cold, dun earth by early frost. The slow pirouette of confrontation that would churn up into this summer's war had just about begun. Kargil was under fire from Pakistani artillery.

Fayaz had driven me up from Srinagar then. A veteran Valley hand, Fayaz was no stranger to peril. But the drive to Kargil had shaken him. When shells began flying between Kharbu and Kaksar, he ducked his head into the steering wheel and stepped on the accelerator. I remember telling him what I would repeat often this summer: ducking inside the car or speeding is no insurance against a flying shell; if it has to get you it will, no matter what the vehicle's speed, or the angle of your body's contortion.

Late one night, Fayaz shook me awake. We were at the Kargil Dak Bungalow and a few shells had flown close over its gables. "Lagta hai kayamat aane waali hai, wapas chaliye," Fayaz told me. He did not want to stay; he wanted to go and never ever come back.

Fayaz was in Kargil again during this summer's war, driving a CNN team; he appeared less afraid and more accepting even though June-July of 1999 in Kargil was much worse than the September of 1998. But the penumbra of the intruder had begun to emerge even on that first trip. One of my reports for *The Telegraph* had said, "For a tribe that so few in the Valley can even claim fleeting familiarity with, they (foreign militants) have built up an awesome reputation. Nobody quite knows them but everybody seems to know of them. They are there, somewhere, probably in the hills and villages up north, and they are up to something. Some say they are launching preparations for a jehad. Others, that they are the apparatchik of a violent insurrection being meticulously planned in Pakistan. Who are these foreign militants? Why are they in Kashmir? Where are they in Kashmir?... A low-intensity response to the shelling from the other side may not quite be the right measure for Kargil... the mounting ferocity of the adversary's posture requires new arrangements."

On my return to Srinagar, a senior state government officer had called me. He thought I was in need of serious advice on my vocation. "I think when journalists have nothing to write, they begin making things up. It is sometimes a good idea not to pay much heed to hearsay. People in Kashmir are idle, they gossip." That evening, at his riverside country home in Ganderbal,

Journeys Without Maps

I told Qayoom, a dear friend and a sensitive Kashmiri, about the officer's counsel. We agreed we were probably being a little morbid about the state of Kashmir but we also agreed we were being realistic. "You will be back soon," Qayoom had told me that night, "Ominous things are going to happen in Kashmir."

A day before I would be back in Kargil, I was in an unlikely place reporting an unlikely story. I was in Goa for Sonia Gandhi's first public appearance since returning as Congress president. I remember opening my copy with a message to the desk: "Here goes the most boring story on earth." Goa was somnolent even though it was Goa Day and a wannabe prime minister was visiting. The voices I recall from that trip were not voices from Goa. They were voices off the television set in my hotel room, waves of expat exhilaration as India beat England at Edgbaston and entered the Super Six of the World Cup. The other voice I remember is of my news editor telling me from Calcutta that Srinagar airport had been reopened, reporters were reaching Kargil.

I spent a night in Mumbai with my parents on the way to the front. My father took me out for coffee in a restaurant he favoured not so much for the coffee but because it had a view of the Arabian sea. We talked late into the evening. That would be my last meeting with him. The night the war officially ended in Kargil, my father died in his faraway city by the sea. Around the time the guns were falling silent on the front, his heart stopped. Pulmonary oedema set off a tide within. He gasped and quickly drowned. He loved the sea.

I got the news the morning after the night of ceasefire. On my numbed journey back to Srinagar to catch a flight, a quaint desire crossed me to ask Ashraf, another driver I used, to stop

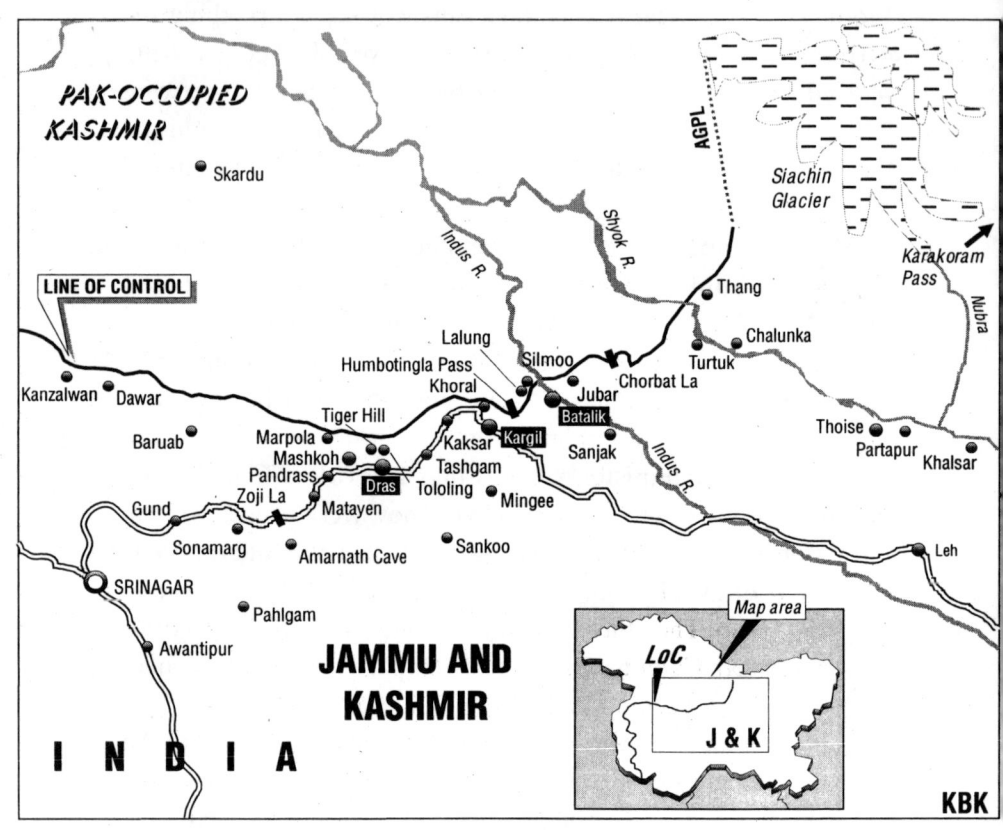

the car so I could pick a few yellow roses. But their season too was over.

Humbotingla: First light has just about broken and the mountains are ringing with what is now their routine wake-up call: the report of shells being fired and shells landing. From a distant meadow, two Bofors guns are tossing lead into the sky and the counterblast is peppering the surrounding hills, columns of smoke and dustcloud lazily rising in the wispy morning light. This is almost too beautiful to be a war.

It was my second day on the front, yet I had seen very little of the war. The road up from Srinagar had been a portentous preview, nothing more. Beyond Sonemarg, National Highway1A (NH1A), the roadlink the intruders were trying to snap to cut Kargil, Leh and Siachen from the rest of India, was a winding ant crawl of troops. Every little clearing beyond Matayen had become a troop bivouac, camouflage netting stretched across tents and ammunition dumps, artillery guns sunk in freshly dug pits, soldiers busy bunkering. Some guns were firing but most were yet to be positioned. Drass was being mercilessly pounded and military convoys were having to race through the devastated town centre. "We are just about settling in," a field major near Drass had said, "this is going to be a long haul." The war was on, of course, but even from the shuddering Drass-Kargil frontier, war, as most of us had come to imagine it, seemed a long, long way away.

I had gone out to the cab stand in the Kargil bazaar looking for a driver who would take me closer to the front, to Batalik perhaps. There wasn't a driver ready and I was just hanging about when a dilapidated Mahindra rattled in belching smoke. The driver peeped out and smiled. "Kahin jaayenge?" (Want to go somewhere?) he asked. I said Batalik and he said yes. This was going to be the first of my many memorable journeys with Ishaq.

The shortest route to Batalik from Kargil was through Humbotingla, a barren pass 13,800 feet high. The road climbed steeply from the Brigade Headquarters, wove past the military helipad and emerged onto a sprawling plain they call the Khurbathang plateau. It was lush with ripening barley and around the plateau's greenery rose high mountains, like forlorn skyscrapers. We were chasing the war but all we saw was beauty unfurling. If Zanskar, just south, was ever the abode of the gods, this would have been its gateway: vast, spare slopes, some burnished rock, some unwrinkled, like sheets spread out, some the soft brownness of chocolate cake. The valleys vanishing below were emerald and streaked with milky streams.

Humbotingla's only inhabitant was a howling, freezing wind. We passed a few artillery positions where Bofors and 130 mm guns had been positioned. A few were booming, and a few were being cleaned with brushes so long they looked like they belonged to Godzilla. The rest was gorgeous desolation.

From the top of Humbotingla we plunged headlong into the Indus gorge via Lalung. Lalung was a quixotic sight: an ochre cluster of cavernous dwellings worked into the hillside, a patch of ancient Judaea transplanted. The terrain changed quickly and in no time we were in the midst of dense apricot forests. We passed orchards of the Silmoo countryside and through more of extravagantly beautiful terrain. Still no signs of the war. When Batalik was just three kilometres on the milestone, I began to suspect that it was all a big lie. That there was no war, no intrusion, no fighting, no death. The road wound down into the craggy gorge and then Ishaq suddenly braked and said, "Batalik, sir."

I wondered if it was some other Batalik we had reached. This couldn't be what was being described in New Delhi's surcharged briefing rooms as the fiercest battleground of Kargil. There wasn't a soul around and the only sound was of the Indus cutting through the rocks a thousand feet below, and of ravens cawing. But Ishaq was smiling the smile of a man who knew better. "Right place but wrong time, sir, the gunfire begins by afternoon and goes on through the night."

Much later, after the commanding officer had let us in and given us what he had promised — "Hot tea and nothing else" — we got our first glimpses of the front. Soldiers wounded in the battle around Jubbar, one of the three embattled ridges above Batalik, were being driven in for air evacuation to Kargil. They were lying on ragged stretchers, wrapped in bloodied bandages and gunny. Some of them were in rather a bad way; their mates held up intravenous drips as they waited for a chopper to take them away. It had clouded over; it was beginning to snow in the upper reaches. Finding a landing site was tough. The soldiers rushed about as more casualties arrived in ambulances. There were only basic medical facilities available at the base; there was little to do but unload the wounded and wait for the chopper.

Columns of soldiers were leaving for the front, slowly inching up the hill tracks in their heavy battle gear — guns, sleeping bags, ammunition, stoves. More batches, grim faced and introspective, were preparing to leave. They had seen the shape of returning parties; they were coming back from the front dead or wounded or scarred. The first waves that went up suffered the worst losses; they had no idea where the enemy was or what he was equipped with. "They had mined the place and they were firing rockets where machine-guns would have done," one junior officer said, "God forbid, if this lasts till the winter, we and the enemy will both be buried by nature."

The Batalik command post had taken heavy shellfire. The pucca barracks had been blown to shreds and the unit had had to scatter itself in the mountain's nooks. Tin and tarpaulin quarters had been erected in narrow rock shelters where the cold wind was a brazen and constant infiltrator. Batalik village — a straight row of homes clinging to sheer mountain face — was empty. Some villagers had padlocked their doors before fleeing to the safety of Silmoo and Lalung; it didn't strike them that artillery never knocks, it just blows through.

Ishaq was right. The shelling began late afternoon on our way back to Kargil to file the day's story. It was mostly blind fire, what the army calls HF, harassment fire. We were stopped at a Bofors position near Apati by a gunner. He was irate. He pulled Ishaq out of his seat without feeling the need to explain himself and began checking the Mahindra's rickety dashboard. We protested about being legitimate people but he had already begun a summary trial.

"Do you have a radio set here?" he asked.

"No, sir." Ishaq was trembling.

"Why do you have tapes in the car?"

"Only to listen to songs sir."

"Are you Shia or Sunni?"

"Shia, sir."

"You don't have a radio set?"

"No, sir."

I asked the soldier what this was all about and he said someone had been radioing gun area locations to the Pakistani side. "This is a new gun position and we are already under fire, the bastards have been told. I'll let you go, but be careful with these fellows.

We distrust Sunnis hundred percent and Shias ninety-nine percent." (Most Kargilis are Shias). He waved us off. I was too embarrassed to even look Ishaq in the eye. It was getting to be a stormy afternoon; dark clouds had gathered and they were bursting with the guns. Ishaq was quiet and nervous. He drove the Mahindra down to Kargil as if he was riding a toboggan and was in urgent need of beating the world mark.

Sanjak: Batalik is the stepchild of the frontier. Drass gets attention because it holds the key to the national highway, supply line to Siachen and Leh. Batalik's only highway is the turbulent Indus which carries only silt and anyway flows into Pakistan.

It was only much later that Ishaq would tell us Batalik was home. As a child he had played in its famed apricot orchards and frolicked in the Indus and the many streams that feed its flow. We had spent too long one evening in Batalik chatting to soldiers returning from the battle for the Muntho Dalo ridge (above Batalik). It was dark by the time we were ready to leave which meant, in effect, that we could not leave.

We had spent most of our time that evening at a forward base hospital. It was a cluster of tattered tents on a ledge where mules roamed and dust ruled. Wounded soldiers stood in a long line before a doctor who sat on a collapsible chair in the open. A few lay in the tents. Most of them had splinter or bullet wounds, but some were simply in shock. A young rifleman had not been able to urinate for a week on the heights. He lay in a tent, bloated, pale and in pain. Another had developed neurotic disorders from the sound of shelling, he could not hold himself up or walk.

They were soldiers of the Jammu and Kashmir Light Infantry (JAKLI), back from the raging battle for the Muntho Dalo ridge. Most of them were Kashmiri Muslims fighting India's war for Kashmir. Later that night I mulled over whether I should make a point of that in my despatch and decided against it. The soldiers were not there proving a special point; they were fighting just like jawans from elsewhere in India. To see something unique in their participation in the war would perhaps have been presumptuous. I, in fact, asked two Kashmiri jawans — Riaz Ahmed and Mohammed Shafi — if fighting Pakistani intruders in Kashmir meant something more to them and the expression on Riaz's snow-scorched face immediately made me realise I had made a horrible mistake. "Would you ask that kind of question to a jawan from Uttar Pradesh or Bihar?"

My mind went back to the Apati gunner and his sour little sermon on trusting Muslims. Kashmir has long been a split-level war — a battle with the enemy within and the enemy without. That sense was constant in Kargil. "This is no ordinary war," the Apati gunner had told us. "We are fighting a hostile enemy from hostile ground. There is little local support. You see, this is not a war for Kargil, this is a war for Kashmir. We have had to fight Kashmiris to keep Kashmir. Trust is a tough thing." More's the pity I had asked that question of JAKLI rifleman Riaz.

It was dark by the time we left the base hospital and there was nowhere to spend the night. Ishaq said he knew people in the area for it was home. He took us to a cottage in Sanjak, a little wooded village across the Indus in Batalik. We arrived late in the night and without prior notice but the large and lovely family of Akbar Khan, a local government contractor, was welcoming. They gave us food — sumptuous chicken curry, spinach and rice —and a warmly carpeted floor. We went down

Journeys Without Maps

to the river for a while and lay across a plank bridge in the dark watching Bofors guns fire across the Batalik frontier. The guns were far away so we couldn't hear them; there was only the sound of military trucks droning and the river running. The shells were little lights silently leaping into the sky and mingling with the stars. They were stunning.

Sanjak would be our first night in many without bedbugs. And the next morning, we would get fresh water from the stream to wash with.

"So this is our Hotel Saigon, isn't it?"

Jaffer had again promised water but as usual it hadn't come. I hadn't bathed in eight days. I was just back from two straight nights in bunkers in Drass and Jaffer had probably taken pity at the horror of my appearance. He had offered two full buckets of it, and hot to boot. But Jaffer's promises were like birds in the bush. He would make a good politician. He was a scoundrel, though an utterly lovable one. He took my carton of cigarettes away one day saying I smoked too much. "I will ration them for you," he said. He also smoked them for me.

The only way around him was to call Ali. Ali himself wasn't the ablest or the most willing bellboy but if you gave him a job Jaffer had failed to do, Ali would most certainly do it. "This is something beyond Jaffer," you had to tell him and Ali could work the magic of Alladin's djinn. And if you called Ali up for jobs too often, it would hurt Jaffer's pride just enough to get him to work.

Mohammed Sadiq Rahi, doughty owner of Kargil's Hotel Siachen and, consequently, employer of Jaffer and Ali, probably played similar games with their egos to squeeze the best out of them. To Ali he gave the honour of being personal valet in addition to hotel bellboy; he cooked his master's meals and slept by his doorstep. Jaffer was the major domo at work, keeper of hotel records, minder of the shack that had the distinction of being labelled the hotel's reception, and scribe of bills and expenses.

Half the problems of staying in Hotel Siachen were solved if you had Jaffer and Ali at your beck and call; the other half even God's angels seemed incapable of doing anything about. Like bugs in the bed that set off such violent itches nobody was embarrassed about scratching in public after a while. Or, the two phone lines that would either not work or were so overworked they frequently collapsed. At any hour of the day, there was someone either dialling a number from that phone or waiting to receive a call. Writing the story of the day was never the end of the job. It was only the beginning of prolonged telephonic agony. And when you did get through, the story had to be screamed out on a line as faint as an eye surgeon's thread.

There were days when one paragraph of the story would go to the Delhi office, another to Calcutta, then one to Delhi again, torn, as the frontier itself. I had been reading Ryszard Kapuscinski's *Another Day of Life* on the Angolan civil war. He had had trouble filing to Warsaw for the Polish News Agency from the depths of Africa but even he seemed better off than some of us in Kargil.

Hotel Siachen was a bed-and-nothing place. Cigarettes and water were not the only things you didn't get there. You didn't even get tea. But for a long time, it was the only place to report the war from. It stood in the pit of one of the many lanes that ran down Kargil's main street, a three-storeyed wood and concrete structure shaped like an inverted L. At the centre of the L was a little patch of soil that was once a garden. There was even a distended sprinkler pitched in the middle.

Journeys Without Maps

So many cigarettes had been thrown into the garden from three tiers of balconies around, it had actually become a huge ashtray. The joke was cigarette trees would sprout from it the next spring and Sadiqbhai would have another shop in Kargil's main bazaar. Other than the hotel, Sadiqbhai owned a shoe store, a stationery outlet and a sports goods shop. Jaffer and Ali had a cricket bat. On lazy forenoons, we would bash the ball about in the little courtyard by the phone room— Associated Press (AP) photographer Saurabh Das and I. Saumya Bandopadhyay of *Ananda Bazar Patrika* would often take a break from his frustrations with the phone and join in. Jaffer shanghaied kids from the bylanes to do the fetching. I broke a few of Siachen's windowpanes. We later bought a football and Saurabh unleashed his magic foot. I was never any good with it. I broke windowpanes again. I suspect that charming rascal called Jaffer worked the cost somewhere into my bills.

Mingee: At the flyblown bus halt in Trespone was a huddle of displaced children, the pink of their cheeks smudged by the dust of travel, their clothes ragged and torn, their little bare feet shrunk on the cold earth, their eyes vacant and askance. What a pretty little ugly war this is.

Ali had his own ways of squeezing money out. Jaffer was an unapologetic grabber who went straight for the purse. Ali went to it through your heart. "My parents and sisters are all very ill, why do you think I am working in the middle of this war? Allahkasam, I would have run away if I could, just give me a little change if you can."

We never got Ali's whole truth but he was probably not entirely lying. He came from Kaksar, which fell in the direct line of fire. Settlements in Kaksar had had to be abandoned; they had all moved,

15

like thousands of others, to villages in the safer Suroo valley south of Kargil — Mingee, Trespone, Pannikhar, Tresgam, Sankoo. There were two reasons why Ali, and most other Kargilis, would always lace their references to Pakistan with expletives: unlike the Valley Muslims, they were Shias who had problems with Sunni Pakistan and who looked to Iran for spiritual and temporal sustenance, and, in the immediate sense, they blamed Pakistan for so horribly dislocating their lives. Kargilis would never lose an opportunity to underline the difference between their and the Valley Muslims' attitude towards Pakistan. The night India beat Pakistan in the cricket World Cup, they went out and burst crackers. Kargil came under spiteful shelling from across after the match ended but the Kargilis kept up the celebrations.

From Pandrass to Kargil, the entire stretch of villages had been uprooted by the invasion; the villagers had fled, old men and women who had lost the comfort of their beds and hearths, children who had been snatched away from school, farmers who had been driven from their land. In Pandrass, the Indian artillery had moved into their homes and dug guns in their courtyards and lanes. In Drass, the homes had all been destroyed, their roofs torn and their walls flattened by shellfire. Only the horses were left, freed of their masters and restored, if only temporarily, to the pristine freedom of open fields.

One morning at a nowhere spot between Mingee and Sankoo village, we stopped the car to meet a cluster of refugees. They turned out to be one big family — Bairam Khan, his three veiled wives, the eleven children he had sired, two frazzled cockerels, three cooking gas cylinders and an eddy of satchels. They were waiting to be picked up but who would host a family so large? Bairam Khan looked distraught; he was cursing the war but he was also probably regretting he married thrice.

Journeys Without Maps

Displaced Kargili children in a makeshift school in Mingee.

Mingee's one-street bazaar was like a crowded railway platform. Both sides of the street were strewn with trunks and holdalls with their owners perched on them. Buses came packed with people from Kargil and beyond, disgorged some and rolled on to off-load remnants of their confused human cargo at points further along the refugee trail.

The Suroo valley stretched miles on the river's spine, bedraggled, and bewitching at the prime of summer bloom. The river's flanks were a procession of flowers and above loomed the shimmering snows of Zanskar. But it was a stained paradise. If the valley was ravishing, it was also ravaged, with thirty-five thousand refugees left wandering.

The hospitals at Kargil and Mingee were deluged with the ill and the injured, mostly unattended. Their staff had either decamped or were on furlough. They had run out of essential medicines. The drains overflowed and refuse piled on street corners. The exhaust of battle was blowing misery into life's humdrum. But for all the tales of woe and anguish that lay strewn in the Suroo valley, the refugees remained a fallback beat for most of us; we would rush to Mingee the day the front did not offer a story.

Drass: "Two hundred artillery guns firing across the mountains all night. Will that make a good story for you?"

This officer shall remain unnamed in the story for reasons that have to do with the strange workings of the defence establishment — the games they can play with good officers and the petty wars they can unleash. But if this man wasn't a good soldier, true to his calling and country, the Indian Army probably doesn't have any. He, more than anyone else, introduced some of us to the face of the war and to the life of the man who wages it: the footsoldier. He showed us how spectacular and how sorry war could be, how exciting and frightening, how necessary and how utterly futile.

He commanded an artillery unit that shuttled about Drass during the two months of conflict. He wore a colonel's rank on his shoulders but he had the heart of a jawan. And he had a mind of his own, which is not always a good thing to have. The Indian Army was still struggling for a foothold in the mountains when we first met him. We had stopped by his gun area on a rocky hillside near Drass one afternoon and by the time we left half an

Journeys Without Maps

hour later, he had extended us an invitation to visit again. "If you want to see the war, come and see it with the soldiers."

It was at his unit that we heard the first horror stories of initial attempts to recapture the heights — stories of boulders being rolled down on hapless Naga soldiers trying to make blind runs up the mountains by night, stories of assault parties being exterminated in ambushes because they had no idea where the enemy lay, stories of jawans arriving from the plains and being sent up heights above eighteen thousand feet in nothing but canvas shoes and cotton jackets. It was at his unit that we got accounts, first hand, of the unpreparedness of the army — of there not being enough guns and men to fight off the intrusion, of there not being enough information about enemy positions, of there not being enough for the soldiers to eat. The first parties moved up without rations. They rubbed snow for water and lived on nothing. When the food did arrive, it was useless. "They sent us puris and subzi. At those heights, puris and subzi freeze to stone, you can't eat any of it," a young officer who had miraculously returned from a reconnaissance mission up an intruder-ridden peak, told us. He had survived on cigarettes and chocolates in his pup tent. "But my poor jawans had virtually nothing to eat, they were eating snow and they were in the open."

Partly because they were so strained and stretched in the early days, and partly because of unstated policy, few officers spoke to journalists. We would set out early from Hotel Siachen on journeys without maps, hoping to run into something. If we got an officer to tell us even a bit of how the battle was going or saw live crossfire, we considered ourselves fortunate. For the most part, the jawans sustained journalism as they sustained the front, quite freely sharing their experiences and apprehensions.

"What drives you?" I once asked a Rajputana Rifles soldier back from the battle for Peak 5140 in Drass, "What makes you

The jawans sustained journalism as they sustained the front, freely sharing their experiences and apprehensions.

go on even though you know you may die the next moment?" He looked at me a bit incredulously and said, "Orders. If we don't follow orders, what will our families eat?" I wondered about big words like patriotism and bravery and the soldier said, "I don't know about that. Perhaps sometimes, when your fellow soldiers die, there is too much anger. It is then a blinding madness, you don't think about death, you just go on."

There were ways of making things easier for the soldier but the government was not prepared. It was not prepared, for instance, to open another front and engage Pakistani attention elsewhere. It was not prepared to let the troops cross the Line of Control (LoC) and operate from behind enemy lines. "The enemy is tearing every norm to shreds, he is free to violate everything, including our borders, but not us. If we are fighting a war let us fight a war. Why aren't we calling this a war? This is a war. We have been invaded, our soldiers are dying, let us fight it like a war. But our government wants to stick to strange rules. You cannot fight a bully if you want the good boy prize." Kargil had made the colonel very angry.

And that was also the sentiment of the soldier across the frontier. He couldn't be bothered about the subtle diplomatic games New Delhi was playing in world capitals. He was in the trench and he wanted to fight back with his arms free. "Let the diplomats pussyfoot, but let soldiers fight like soldiers." Similar murmurs rose when, weeks later, a ceasefire was suddenly called and the intruders allowed safe passage. "If we did have to let them walk back in peace, why have so many of our soldiers killed," a jawan from the Jat regiment would say in Kaksar, midway between Kargil and Drass. "Now was the time to have taught them a lesson so they would think many times before repeating this. We have let them go scot free, they will needle us again."

It was from the colonel's unit too that we witnessed the first Indian success of the war: the taking of Tololing. Two nights before the final assault, the colonel had winked and said, "Come the day after, you'll probably see what you've never seen before."

It was the night of smoke on earth and fire in the sky. Twenty-five artillery units pounded snow-streaked Tololing from three directions: Kaksar, Drass and Matayen. Twenty thousand artillery shells or more were fired that night and by morning, Tololing had been pulverised into submission. The firing began as dusk dissipated into darkness. The first to go were the Bofors guns, coughing TNT from positions all across NH1A. Then came a barrage of medium range fire from 130 mm and 105 mm guns.

The shells were vaulting into the sky and then plummeting over Tololing and beyond. It was a cosmic strobe show, the skies flashing and booming with gunfire. And then, as the darkness thickened, Russian-built multi-barrel rocket launchers exhaled fire, like dragons spitting.

We drove to another gun area in the colonel's jonga. The vicinity was shaking with the report of heavy guns. Sound blasts rippled through the jonga and its undercarriage rattled as if it were about to be torn asunder. The guns were shrouded in dust and fumes and the gunners scurried about, sinister shadows in the gathering pall, feeding the guns and firing. Later we climbed into a stationary truck which was the field operations room. We heard infantry parties closing in on Tololing directing artillery fire and reporting progress on the radio. "We'll get them tonight," said the officer in charge, "this kind of massed artillery action is too much for them to sustain."

We went to sleep awhile in an empty tent on the hillside— it fluttered like a paper ball in the gale all night, perilously close to being blown away — and when we woke up, the unit was already celebrating. "We got them, we got them, we knocked the fellows off Tololing," cried the officer from the operations room truck. His eyes were bloodshot and bleary from nightlong action but a smile was spreading on his face.

The morning air was thick with pungent gun smoke and the hillside was littered with the debris of a harsh night: scattered brass gunshells, fatigued, soot-ridden gunners sprawled in their pits, the earth under the guns lacerated with tyre treads. "Even this looks like a battleground," the colonel said, "imagine what it must look like where our fire landed."

After Tololing, the Indian military campaign went hill-hopping in Drass, one peak after another until Tiger Hill was taken three

Journeys Without Maps

weeks later. Drass would become a daily beat — it offered the best spectator seats on the war for the heights. From the centre of the shelled out, abandoned hamlet you had a panavision view of the embattled peaks: Tiger Hill to the extreme left, still streaked with snow in midsummer, then Peak 5140, a lofty grey mountain with broad flanks, and, to the extreme right, Tololing, a craggy peak with down to earth contours, the kind schoolchildren sketch in their drawing books.

On a good day, Drass was barely three hours from Kargil. The winding up-and-down ride to Chhenigund, and then the race through Kaksar-Kharbu belt, which was within sight of Pakistani gun positions and which popped with shellfire like a popcorn bowl. The road was a thin strip that rose and dipped along the Drass nullah; if you were hit, you either got plastered to the hill side or were washed away in the current. Beyond Kharbu, the road opened into lovely country, dappled with meadows and gullies overrun by yellow roses. A little short of Drass ran the Bimbet nullah, a cold, crystal seductress of a stream in which I would promise myself a bath every time we crossed it.

The authors of Operation Vijay have shut the media's window on this raging undeclared war for unmanned territory. This remains an embattled front but its story cannot be told because its raconteurs have been ordered to silence.

The curtain fell almost too abruptly. The colonel sent his second-in-command to our hotel rooms in Kargil very early one morning with an apologetic but firm request: he wanted the cardboard shell cases he had signed for us as mementos of war and friendship. "There cannot be any record we met, the colonel is very very sorry but he wants the cases back," the embarrassed 2IC said. He looked worried and he was in a great hurry. "I must get back before it is light. Please don't mention to anyone we even met. We don't know you, you don't know us. Military Intelligence (MI) has been snooping and asking questions about media visits to our gun area. Perhaps there will be a court of inquiry."

He was one of the officers who had conducted the successful assault on Tololing, one among the men who had brought back the country's first trophy of the war. But one visit by an intelligence cop in mufti armed with nothing more than a notebook and a few awkward questions had reduced him to nervous trembling.

Over the next few days news sources ran out like fluid through a funnel. We were barred from entering field brigades. Movement was made difficult with checks every few hundred metres. Even friendly officers either made themselves unavailable or politely excused themselves. "Sorry, orders." The army did not want to begin expelling journalists from the frontier — that would have been bad PR — but it had resorted to a slow burnout operation. It had stopped honouring its own media permits, it would not allow journalists who left Kargil to return. MI and local police cops were sent out on little harassment trips to Hotel Siachen: they would daily want to know our names, our addresses, our sources, our plans, even our "purpose of visit", as if we were there researching features on angling in Kargil's streams.

Hotel Siachen became a sorry citadel. Quite suddenly, there were just six of us left — Saurabh and his correspondent colleague from AP, Hema Shukla, Gaurav Sawant of *The Indian Express*, Saumya of *Ananda Bazar Patrika* and his rival from *Bartaman*, Musarraf Hussain, and I. Saumya's and Musarraf's newspapers were bitter rivals in Calcutta but in Kargil the two maintained a strange competitive camaraderie. They were perhaps in such desperate need to know what the other was upto that they had decided to stick together — perhaps that way they didn't waste time spying on each other.

Then the Calcutta twins left too and we were just four. We hung together, like survivors of a shake out. My motives in being part of a team were perhaps most selfish. The phone lines from Kargil had suddenly died — part of the unofficial censorship, we surmised — and Gaurav and I were desperate. The only way of sending stories through was the AP satellite phone and even before we could ask, Hema had graciously offered it. It didn't just mean using the satphone, it also meant Hema scrunching her filing time on the laptop and adjusting to our deadline schedules, and Saurabh having to set up connections several times over. But for the two of them, I would have had to pack my bags within a week. Neelesh Misra, a shy young poet from Lucknow who also doubled as AP's correspondent and came to Kargil to replace Hema, honoured the favour.

It was a strange time to impose a news blackout. Indian forces were on a roll. Tololing had been taken and recapturing the remaining peaks in Drass was a matter of time. Troops were in the process of getting an upper hand in Batalik and in Turtuk, the threat of insurrection had been neutralised by the Ladakh Scouts. The defence ministry briefings in New Delhi were getting progressively assured and aggressive and, in the fourth week of battle, they didn't sound terribly disconsonant with what was happening on the ground. Now was the time, if any, to open the front to the media. We would discuss the bizarre policy of the Government of India with a mixture of stupefaction and glee. After all, the media squeeze had left the whole field open to just a handful of us who had happened to stay on.

For most of us, Kargil was the biggest story we had been on. It didn't take the daily whoops of the youthful Gaurav Sawant — "Guys, guys, I'm so thrilled it's my thirty-third front page byline in a row, I've never had it so good" — to make us realise this. War hadn't ever happened between two nuclear powers. And this war had happened to everybody — the army and the media — quite suddenly, without chance for preparation. Initially, and fortuitously for some of us, the army was too busy getting its act together to bother about the media. They tried to impose restrictions for a while but realised they would be better served by organised media exposure. Kargil became the most freely reported war — and the first televised one — on the subcontinent.

The ban was lifted as inexplicably as it had been imposed — after a fortnight or so. Suddenly, the army began bringing in busfulls of journalists from Srinagar. Overnight, everything changed. Camera crews were roving where they wouldn't even allow people with pens and notebooks. The government had realised it had a propaganda war to fight too.

The conducted media parties came and receded like tides. Hotel Siachen would turn into a merry Tower of Babel for two nights a week. The mornings were a cacophony of calls for water and fresh towels from the balconies and the exhaust of cars leaving, the evenings a slow crescendo of decibels, rising peg by peg, again from the balconies. Everyone was on the same story but everyone had a different tale to tell. Kargil was a kaleidoscopic frontier. People could have sweltered in the heat of Drass and frozen in the winds of Matayen on the same day; some could have seen victory on the march, some terrible losses. By late evening, Hotel Siachen's balustrades would be dripping over with anecdotes. The night of the ceasefire, a few journalists burst into rapturous celebrations on the balconies. "India zindabad, jai India," rose

Journeys Without Maps

their jubilant cries, "we've knocked the bastards off...they won't dare peep into Kashmir for a while." They were drinking and dancing and hugging each other. "We've done it, we've done it yet again, taught those fellows a good lesson." But Kargil, like Kashmir, was too torn a place for celebrations of any kind; celebrations never came without a sense of guilt. From my room on the second floor of Hotel Siachen that night, I saw people dance in joy and people shrink into dark corners. For instance, Ashraf, the driver.

Ashraf was a Valley Muslim, a Sunni and a closet Pakistan-sympathiser. He had come to Kargil as AP's driver from Srinagar and stayed on much longer than he had imagined, not because he wanted to but because his job demanded that. It was never quite clear what he made of the whole war but he made it evident he wasn't on the side of the Indians. The night of the India-Pakistan World Cup match, he slunk out of our hotel room the moment it became apparent Pakistan would lose. Ashraf was a child of the "azaadi" movement; India was an evil presence in his life. Kargil though wasn't really something he was involved in. On the night of the ceasefire, amid the celebrations on the balconies of Hotel Siachen, he let down his guard a bit. "The Pakistanis are retreating? From Kashmir? Really?" he remarked sardonically when I went down to meet him; it was not something he wanted to believe.

Trust is tough in Kashmir and both sides have good reason not to trust. This is not a black and white story; it is grey and very grim. One late night on a gun position in Drass, when the war was at its peak and rum had again inured us to shellfire and plunged us into the temporary vortex of bluntness, the old debate re-emerged from the confines of politeness. A few army officers began complaining that the media was "not supporting" the war effort, just as they had been complaining that the media had not supported the anti-insurgency drive in Jammu & Kashmir; it had turned "anti-state" by reporting excesses by security forces. One of them referred to a report I had written from the front about the tremendous odds Indian jawans were up against and said, "Do you know that report has hurt the national interest? It has hurt the jawans' morale?" No jawan on the front was getting to read *The Telegraph*, or any other newspaper. The only thing the report had probably hurt was the defence establishment because it showed them up as unprepared for the enemy and uncaring for its own soldiers. The officer spoke as if the interests of the defence establishment were the same as the "national interest", just as governments tend to confuse their interest with the national interest.

We saw only one side of the war and most stories we reported were stories told to us by Indian soldiers. A lot of what the jawans had to say mismatched with what the defence establishment thought. Accounts of how well-entrenched the intruders were, for instance; that was anathema to the government because it was handy proof it had let its guard down. Accounts, also, of how our own soldiers treated intruders when they could lay their hands on them. New Delhi made quite a show of the mutilation of some of its captured solidiers by the Pakistanis but much the same was happening on this side. Troops of the Naga and Jat regiments told us quite plainly they had killed a few intruders they had captured alive in the heights above Drass. "It was rage, just rage," one Naga soldier said, "They had killed many of our mates, we were angry. When we got them, we butchered them." As and when they brought bodies of intruders back from the heights, they tied them with ropes and dragged them down. "We had enough load to carry as it was, who was going to bother carrying their bodies? Dragging them down was a favour." There was no sense of guilt or remorse there, just plain retelling; it was as if a fire of emotion had cleansed the act of murder.

Mushkoh: In the end they just become dead weights loaded on the backs of unknowing mules, their dignity wrapped in tattered blankets. If they are fortunate, these blankets will somewhere have a little badge of honour pinned, an inch of metal for miles of motherland.

Brigade-Major Rajeev Srivastava was in no mood to receive us. We had arrived at his camp deep in the Mushkoh valley uninvited and unannounced. He was busy and he could well have sent us back. But he had ushered

"What does the jawan get out of this war?" asked the brigade-major. "If he dies he stops getting even the pittance he earns as salary."

us into his tent and ordered tea. He was hard at work on an unsteady little desk piled up with files and papers. The tent was steaming like a sauna in mid-afternoon. "How have you managed to come here?" he asked, scribbling on furiously. "My orders are to allow no media personnel here. If they reach here, I have orders to escort them to Sonemarg, right out of the war zone."

We mildly mentioned our permits and that we were not there to intrude, only to watch the war and write about it, whatever of it we could see and learn about. Then Neelesh — who later discovered a handy Lucknow link with the brigade-major —- said something that touched a raw nerve in him. "Actually we just want to see what the jawans are up against," he ventured, "Essentially we want to talk about their problems."

The brigade-major looked up again from behind the paper piles. "What does the jawan get out of this?" he asked. He was suddenly shaking. "Tell me what does the jawan get? You get your story, we get our quotes in the newspapers, what does the poor jawan get? If he dies, he stops getting even the pittance he earns as salary." It was like a dam had burst somewhere inside him. Tears were quivering in his eyes. He had been drafting commendation letters for soldiers killed in the fighting for the Mushkoh ridges. He had personally sent some of them off to the front. It was a terrible moment. "I'd rather not sign these commendations," he said, "I'd rather have my men back."

He was no longer keen on packing us off. He took us down into a bunker which was the camp's infirmary. It was full of wounded soldiers. In an adjoining room lay a few dead, wrapped in blankets. It was only the third day of battle in Mushkoh but the camp was already brimming over with grim news. It was the same story as elsewhere: the intruders had the advantage of heights, they were heavily armed and well protected, the first Indian

Journeys Without Maps

A wounded Indian soldier in Mushkoh valley.

parties going up had little idea of their positions. Towards twilight, soldiers began silently gathering at the foot of the hill overlooking the camp; jawans from the front were coming down in streaks. Some of them were wounded. They were bleeding from bullet and shrapnel hits but they were still hurtling down. A few too badly hit to walk were being brought down on stretchers. Those who had escaped injury weren't in terribly good shape. Their eyes were bleary, their general countenance quite delirious. Quiet descended on the camp. "This happens every evening when the platoons come back," the brigade-major said, "it is very depressing. They are all what we call the walking-wounded, they might be very seriously hurt, but they have to walk back. We have again underestimated the enemy, this is going to be quite a killing field."

Mushkoh is not much of a valley. It is more a rock-strewn highland that gradually creeps up the heights where lies the invisible LoC. The track to Mushkoh forks off NH1A between Drass and Pandrass and quickly climbs onto a small plain dotted with abandoned settlements. The peaks of Drass had been cleared and the heavy guns were now being sent into Mushkoh. They were rumbling past the hamlets and little causeways and settling down at vantage positions in the new theatre of battle. Soldiers were scattered everywhere, like mountain goats on grass.

We were back in Mushkoh the next afternoon. If guns were jamming the highland, so were television crews and photographers and reporters. Mushkoh had become our Drass. We kept going back after wink-and-shower breaks in Hotel Siachen. That afternoon, as we were having lunch with a bunch of soldiers in a bunker, news arrived of the capture of Pimple II, a peak that had defied assaults. Pimple II was the second success in two days after the taking of Peak 4875. The soldiers cheered, but only briefly. The field phone had also brought news of high casualties.

Journeys Without Maps

The injured and the dead were trickling down the hills slowly on foot and on mule back.

Later, Saurabh and I climbed halfway up the hill to meet another platoon bringing back recoveries from captured positions: broken guns, transmitters, boxfulls of anti-personnel mines, Pakistani Army identity cards, detailed jottings of Indian gun positions, area maps of the Kargil sector, unscrambled codes and radio frequencies the Indian Army was using. "The bastards know everything, down to our codes and gun areas," exclaimed an officer as he spread out the recoveries in his tent, "No wonder they are taking the lives out of us even though we are eventually going to win."

We stayed on in Mushkoh one night. It had begun to rain and a freezing wind was blowing. We were in the cosiness of an officer's snow tent eating dinner when news of the ceasefire arrived. "This isn't good news," the officer said, "we are letting them go when they are on the run, we are letting them off the hook." The guns were still firing; splinters were swooping low over the camp. "You see, by the end of September, there is thirty feet of snow where we are now. If we just let them go, we have to maintain a stricter vigil here, and how are we going to do that through the winter?" He seemed quite aghast and angry at the order to silence his guns.

The firing from across would not stop; it seemed to be getting more belligerent as the night wore on. We had to leave Mushkoh. The officer hadn't a spare tent or a bunker and the shellfire was coming right over the camp. "You have to go," he said. We left at two in the morning — Saurabh, Neelesh and I with a very frightened and cantankerous Ashraf in the driver's seat. He could not switch his headlights on — "Too risky, they may spot you and fire" — so we rode the rubble-strip in the dark. When Ashraf couldn't see a thing — it was rainy and foggy — we flashed a torch to pick the road. We reached Hotel Siachen three hours later, just as light was breaking. We were all in one piece but Ashraf's mood was more menacing than all the guns.

I did not notice the seductions of Bimbet on the dazed dash to Srinagar to catch a flight to Mumbai. And the yellow roses had gone to sleep for the season. But the guns over Mushkoh were still firing. The Kashmir frontier hadn't yet fallen silent.

SELECTIVE TRUTHS

■ PAMELA CONSTABLE

> The South Asia bureau chief of *The Washington Post* was in the privileged position of being able to report from both sides of the Line of Control, apart from the Kashmir Valley. She tries to make sense out of competing versions of elusive truths.

Selective Truths

Kashmir? Not much happening there, just the same intractable dispute everyone has been writing about for years. No need to put it at the top of your list. This was more or less the advice I was given as I set out from Washington early this April for my new assignment covering South Asia, and was trying to set priorities for my first months on the job.

I never could have imagined that, literally within weeks, I would be dodging Pakistani shells in the verdant Mushkoh valley with a squad of Sikh soldiers, interviewing Kashmiri teenagers in Muzaffarabad who dreamed of killing Indian troops and dying for the glory of Islam, touring a Kashmir Valley village that had just been burned to the ground by Indian security forces — or bathing with buckets of cold water by candlelight in a Kargil hotel.

Throughout June and July, I air-hopped between New Delhi and Islamabad, navigated around chugging army convoys on the breathtakingly beautiful but precarious and twisting highway between Srinagar and Kargil, and tried to get as close as possible to the fighting from both sides of the Line of Control (LoC) that separates Indian and Pakistani Kashmir.

I never did witness any actual combat, and I never did reach any definitive conclusions about just who was up in those impenetrable mountains with prosaic names like Point 4100, firing down at the Indian troops who struggled up rockface after icy, near-vertical rockface, trying to dislodge an invisible, anonymous Enemy that had managed to humiliate the fourth largest military establishment in the world.

But during those exhausting and frenetic weeks, I did learn a greal deal about perception and reality, about competing official versions of elusive truths, and about the frightening ease with which objective news coverage can lapse into unquestioning jingoism when issues of patriotism and national security are raised

— even in a flourishing democracy like India with a huge and freewheeling press corps that routinely hoots down prevaricating politicians and leaps on official scandals with gusto.

I also learned something about the prejudices and fears that can linger just beneath the surface of civilised relationships between ethnic and religious groups, and about warring territorial and religious agendas that can completely overlook the desires and concerns of their purported beneficiaries — in this case, the people of Kashmir. I learned about brutality exercised in the name of both liberation and protection, about the manipulation and perversion of impassioned causes, and about the stubborn resistance of historical disputes to solutions that seem, to a newcomer and outsider, logical and long overdue.

The most jarring and immediate contradiction for a journalist to grapple with came in the duelling press briefings offered day after day during June and July by civilian and military authorities in New Delhi and Islamabad. Their casualty figures were wildly divergent, their battlefield descriptions might as well have been depicting two different wars, and their analysis of the causes of the Kashmir conflict and Indo-Pak relations harkened depressingly back to diametrically opposed versions of half-century-old events.

During more than a decade as a foreign correspondent, I had covered guerilla conflicts in El Salvador and Peru, military dictatorships in Chile and Argentina, and a *coup d'etat* in Haiti. I had reported from the Philippines during the last days of Ferdinand Marcos, from South Korea during the pro-democracy student riots, from the Soviet Union in the final days of communist rule, and from Cuba during a decade of intermittent repression and permissiveness towards economic and political freedoms. I had listened to countless lies and selective truths by authorities in a dozen countries, including my own. I had learned to question the official versions of violence and death, to assume that everyone was exaggerating and that no one really wanted press coverage to be "fair" — they wanted it to favour their position.

The difference was that in most of these places and circumstances, I was able to witness for myself what was happening and draw my own conclusions. In Chile, the military might dismiss a charge of torture as "communist propaganda", but I could visit the Catholic church human rights office for testimony and photographs to prove it. In Cuba, authorities might claim they did not harrass political dissidents, but I would visit their homes at night and hear their first-hand stories of being squeezed out of jobs, of being jeered at by organised street mobs, and of being repeatedly detained on frivolous charges. In El Salvador, the government might deny having bombed a village, but peasants from nearby would welcome reporters and show them the charred ruins.

Here, however, I was trying to cover a conflict I could neither see nor hear. I was supposed to describe combat taking place on frozen and inaccessible mountains — terrain that was impossible even to show accurately on a map. I was totally dependent on the carefully orchestrated packaging of two very professional and persuasive sets of officials — whose principal mission was to destroy each other's credibility. How, then, was it possible to begin to learn the truth?

What made it even harder to distinguish fact from fiction was that one side would not even acknowledge it was involved in the fighting in Kargil. Pakistani authorities insisted for weeks that the combatants were independent Kashmiri freedom fighters. India repeatedly insisted the troops were largely Pakistani soldiers in ethnic disguise, and as the conflict continued, they produced large amounts of evidence to support their claim: rounds of ammunition and grenades with Pakistani markings, soldiers' pay books and letters from their loved ones in Urdu, even a wallet with pictures of Pakistani cricket champions. But for weeks they never produced a single prisoner of war or a corpse that could be positively identified as a Pakistani soldier. (It would not emerge until later that many of the fighters had been Pakistani soldiers.) What were we to believe?

Indian authorities also asserted that the Pakistani fighters were committing gruesome atrocities in the heights, while dismissing scattered reports of Indian troops breaking captives' arms and legs atop remote peaks or displaying severed enemy heads in Drass. Instead, officials insisted that India treated the wounded and dead from the opposing side with due respect and protocol. In July, the Ministry of Defence flew a group of journalists from Delhi to Drass to view a Muslim burial ritual for several bodies they claimed were Pakistani soldiers whom Islamabad refused to acknowledge or accept. In contrast, senior officials sombrely announced one day in June that the bodies of six Indian troops had been returned by Pakistan with signs of mutilation and torture — but Pakistan vehemently denied the charge, and again, India produced no corpses or autopsy reports to prove it. What were we to believe?

If the Indian press had any doubts about such charges, it virtually stifled them in the name of wartime patriotism. Instead, the country's leading newspapers and magazines embarked on an unabashedly pro-government campaign to outdo each other in sensational and sentimental coverage of the war. Soldiers' funerals were reported in fulsome detail, funds for Kargil widows and orphans were touted on Page One day after day, and

Selective Truths

advertisers swiftly cashed in on the war fever, creating bellicose slogans and images for products from insecticide to jewellery to insurance. (In an ironic role reversal, the Pakistani press, which is much less free than India's and faces frequent harrassment from authorities, was far more critical of its government's unpopular handling of the Kargil conflict.)

Of course, foreign reporters like myself enjoyed a luxury of perspective unavailable to either Indian or Pakistani journalists; for one thing, we had both professional and diplomatic license to observe and tell both sides of the story, whereas they had access to only one side. (India and Pakistan allow only a few reporters from the other country to visit or live there, and their travels and activities are circumscribed.) For another, we had no native allegiance to either party in the conflict, and could therefore afford to write stories or pursue angles that local journalists, under pressure from editors and publishers to support the war effort, either could or would not touch.

To a large extent, though, we were all subject to the same frustrations of trying to cover a war from antiseptic, remote locations — except when it served either government's purpose to assist us. In late May, when an Indian MiG fighter plane was shot down just inside Pakistani Kashmir, the Pakistani Army arranged within hours to fly a group of journalists to the area in a helicopter. After a long jeep ride and a brief trek through rocky terrain at about twelve thousand feet, we located the wreckage. Dutifully, we snapped photos of Pakistani soldiers holding up the plane's tail, with an Indian flag unmistakably emblazoned on it and the army's regional commander standing smartly alongside in his crisp khakis and beret.

(A week or two later, I was dining with a Pakistani diplomat in New Delhi and showed him my snapshots of the commander and his helicopter crew. The man blanched and gave me a sharp, quizzical look. Then he sighed and told me: the same helicopter had just crashed, in the same mountains, in dense fog. The commander and his entire crew had been killed. I was so shaken I couldn't sleep that night, or the next. I kept seeing an image of the young army pilot, laughing as he showed me the cockpit controls of the big green chopper, stubbing out a cigarette in a can next to his ejection seat, and dismissing my fears of low-altitude mountain flying with a confident wave of his gloved hand.)

The Indian government, after an initial period of prohibiting all journalists from the war zone, also finally relented and offered a series of brief, escorted bus trips to Kargil. Since there was little alternative, I signed up for the first one, and so early one June morning I found myself jolting along one of the most beautiful roads I had ever seen: the highway from Srinagar to Kargil. At first, as we wound upwards past shimmering rice paddies and lush orchards, I couldn't believe I was en route to a war. Kashmiri women in headscarves and earrings squatted in the doorways of chalet-like huts; old men puffed on hookahs in store fronts; nomad families plodded along, driving herds of small bleating goats.

As we climbed higher, though, more ominous signs appeared. Soldiers in camouflage uniforms began stopping us at bridges and crossroads. Caravans of gaily painted cargo trucks chugged along, loaded with fuel and food for the troops. Artillery nests suddenly appeared beside rushing glacial streams; the gleaming tan barrels of fat Bofors guns poked out from beneath camouflage netting. Suddenly we realised that the villages were deserted — there were no children smiling shyly from doorways; no cows being prodded along with sticks; no dogs napping beside the road. Occasionally we heard a soft boom in the distance, and we realised that just beyond the rows of jagged ridges to our north lay Pakistan. The sound was Pakistani shelling, and it was aimed towards the highway we were travelling on.

That evening, not a little shaken, we reached Kargil. The town was deserted and plunged in blackness. We stumbled into an empty hotel courtyard and rousted the astonished proprietor, who warned us he had no hot water, no electricity, no working telephone, and no food. We said that was just fine, and for the next week we made Hotel Siachen our home, hanging laundry from the balconies, bathing in buckets of cold water, eating dal and rice from sidewalk stalls and scribbling stories by candlelight. In a way, the primitive conditions made me feel closer to the invisible warriors struggling up those peaks, sleeping on rocks and fighting off the cold. But every time we heard the soft boom of another shell exploding nearby, especially in the deep of night, my heart stopped.

The official excursion was short, tightly controlled and virtually useless. We were given vague briefings by senior staff officers who offered no detailed accounts of the fighting, and we were told we could not speak with any soldiers or officers who had actually been in the Kargil heights. We were driven to remote artillery positions and allowed to photograph guns firing towards Pakistan, but we were given no time to speak with the men stationed there. And within forty-eight hours, we were expected to return to Srinagar.

Feeling frustrated and empty handed, a few of us decided to remain behind and see how much we could observe on our own — and to their credit the army public relations officers did not force us to leave. Witnessing mountain-top combat was still impossible, but there were plenty of soldiers to chat with as we wandered through the war zone that week and on another visit in July. The jawans were everywhere — waiting for truck convoys to move them to the front; standing in endless lines in public phone booths to call their families from Kargil; cleaning artillery equipment beside rivers along the highway; catching up on badly-needed rest on sleeping bags in Drass.

Even in brief conversations, the solders' sense of pride and patriotic duty was immediately evident. They expressed anger at India's initial humiliation in the hills, deep mistrust of Pakistan, and a strong desire for revenge. I met soldiers from Tamil Nadu to Assam; I met Hindus, Sikhs and even a few Muslims — and all seemed united by the challenge of fighting a common enemy. In some cases, though, the soldiers also confided a visceral antipathy to what they viewed as a foreign Islamic conspiracy against India, as well as a burning frustration that they were under orders to play by the rules and not cross the LoC — while Pakistan had sent hundreds of fighters into Indian territory. "I wish we could just go in there, fight a real war with Pakistan, and get this over with once and for all," one soldier told me.

The combat troops and officers I met were uniformly laconic about the conditions they were enduring on the grim, icy ridges. One squad of soldiers from the Rajputana Rifles, flopping exhausted on sleeping bags in an abandoned storefront in Drass, was resting after two weeks on Tololing ridge, a key peak that India had just captured. "It was snowing the whole time," said one soldier with wind-burned cheeks and bloodshot eyes. He made heavy panting motions with his chest. "You couldn't walk more than a few metres without stopping to breathe." In a nearby roadside camp, a signal corpsman offered us tea and crisp breakfast puris. He had trekked fourteen hours carrying radio equipment up the slopes of Tiger Hill, he said, and got lost in the snow. "I prayed that I would survive, and I did," he said simply.

Selective Truths

The civilian population — a mixture of Shiite Muslims with posters of Iranian mullahs on their walls, Ladakhi Buddhists, Kashmiri merchants, Nepalese refugees, and mountain peasants — seemed to adjust to the war with familiar, stoic resignation. Living so near the LoC, they had long become accustomed to shells echoing and landing in the hills nearby. One morning in the marketplace, we heard a series of shuddering booms closer than usual. Old men in shop fronts looked up briefly from their hookahs, children grabbed at their mothers' hands, and a cow or two started nervously. Eyes anxiously scanned the horizon, and fingers pointed at several puffs of smoke where the shells had landed. Then, after a moment, everyone went back to haggling over eggs and cherries and soap.

For the thousands of war-zone villagers who had been evacuated by the army and relocated on the outskirts of Kargil, though, every day seemed a struggle between boredom and despair. Most had been taken in by local families, where they were crammed into spare rooms and sheds. They had left their animals and their crops behind unattended. Their children had nothing to do, so a few teachers set up makeshift schools in the fields. The women busied themselves with cooking and washing, but the men mostly squatted along the roadside, murmuring among themselves and frowning with worry.

One day in July, four of us ventured by jeep into the Mushkoh valley, a verdant riverside region just northwest of Drass that had been evacuated by the army and was strictly off limits to journalists. As we drove through several villages, the silence was eerie, and we saw no one except a platoon of Sikh soldiers with pack horses, loading supplies of milk, batteries and curried cauliflower to carry to a base camp part way up the Tiger Hill. Then, across a deserted field, we noticed half a dozen men trudging along in ragged clothes. They explained they were local farmers who had just returned to the valley from Kargil for the first time since May, hoping to learn what had become of the homes and animals they left behind. One man said he had owned sixty sheep, and now he feared all were lost, possibly eaten by wolves. "My whole life is gone," he said.

Moments later, we heard the telltale sounds of soft thunder from the north, and suddenly Pakistani shells were raining down around our jeep — the only vehicle visible for miles. As the fifth shell exploded on a nearby hill, we scrambled for the jeep and raced back to the highway. Behind us, the farmers turned and resumed their mission, trudging patiently towards a cluster of grazing cows as the startled beasts scattered across the stony field.

From the other side of the LoC, the story was equally haunting. During June and July, I made several trips to Pakistani Kashmir, where I glimpsed the destruction wrought by Indian shelling, the deeply entrenched anger of communities exiled from their homeland across the border, and the chilling, soft-spoken fanaticism of young Islamic militants who had vowed to defeat the Indian oppressors in Kashmir or meet death in the attempt. It was a strange place; grim and intense, obsessed with religion and political revenge; with little sign of the warmth and elasticity that seemed to characterise Muslim society in Indian Kashmir.

After one long and nauseating jeep ride up to the Bhimbar hills region along the border, I found myself ushered into the homes of Kashmiri villagers who had been killed by Indian shells. In separate rooms, the men and women gathered to mourn, kneeling next to piles of prayer-counting pebbles, swaying silently while a visiting Muslim cleric intoned a prayer for the dead in Arabic.

Selective Truths

A newly-married young woman mourns the death of her father in Indian shelling on the Pakistani side of the LoC.

One young woman, her face contorted in grief, told me her father had just travelled home from his job as a labourer in the Middle East to attend her wedding; less than a week after the ceremony he was killed by a shell in his front yard.

It was easy to sympathise with civilians who had lost their loved ones, of course; it was far more difficult to know or understand the feelings of the men who had gone off to fight against Indian forces in Kargil or the Kashmir Valley. They were truly an invisible army, unnamed and unheralded by the Pakistani press while India's "brave jawans" were grinning stoically on Indian magazine covers. Their dead were buried or left on icy mountain ridges, while fallen Indian troops were honoured with floral wreaths and trumpet fanfares. Indian authorities dismissed

Pakistanis holding Indian shells on their side of the LoC.

the infiltrators as a mishmash of foreign mercenaries, Islamic fanatics, and callow Pakistani troops forced into combat. Pakistani authorities called them freedom fighters worthy of moral and diplomatic support — and yet for reasons of political expedience, professed to know almost nothing about them.

Selective Truths

For ordinary Pakistanis, as well, the war in Kargil seemed a remote and abstract campaign; an issue they cared about as a symbol of national honour, but not an event they could relate to personally. While India's fighters hailed from hometowns across the nation, Pakistani fighters were either unidentified or, as it turned out, mostly members of the Northern Light Infantry

The ordinary Pakistani was too preoccupied with his daily struggle for survival to focus on the Kargil war.

from the isolated border region of Pakistan. Still, many Pakistanis professed support for the incursion and, later, there was a widespread outpouring of dismay and disgust that Prime Minister Nawaz Sharif had bowed to American pressure to call it off. In cities like Karachi and Peshawar, where Islamic fundamental influence is strong, people expressed passionate support for the mujahideen and their latest venture, be it sabotaging army patrols in Srinagar or capturing mountains in Kargil.

But for the most part, Pakistanis were too preoccupied with their own daily struggle for survival to focus much on the distant fighting. In a city like Rawalpindi, a teeming scene of broken-down tonga wagons, fuming buses, bazaars, beggars and children lugging garbage sacks, many people said they were far more concerned about such issues as government corruption, poor public schools, a gaping lack of jobs and the country's desperate economic conditions. One father of nine, who had come by bus from his village in a futile effort to find a job, said his one priority in life was obtaining drinking water for his family. Another man, a well-educated oil company employee, said he kept a car outside his house for show but had to skip meals often in order to pay for his children to attend a decent school.

It was only when I met with the militants themselves, some in Muzaffarabad and others in their headquarters in Islamabad, that I finally got a glimpse of the powerful, self-abnegating conviction that drove the Islamic separatist insurgency. Some of what they said sounded noble and inspired; some of it sent chills down my spine. In a run-down house in downtown Islamabad with sandals scattered around the front door, I met both officials and recruits of one longtime insurgent group, Lashkar-e-Taiba. The leaders of Lashkar, a pan-Islamic

Selective Truths

The writing is on the wall in Muzaffarabad.

organisation that had been deeply involved in the Afghan war against the Soviet Union, were evasive about their relationship with Pakistani security agencies, but open about their multiple motives and goals in Kashmir.

"We took up arms to liberate Kashmir from the tentacles of Indian occupation. They call us terrorists, but the real terrorists are the Hindus who blasphemed our mosques and burned down our houses," said Hafiz Mohammad Saeed, the greying and myopic Muslim cleric who heads Lashkar — and who said he had lost thirty-six relatives to the communal violence that accompanied Partition in 1947. "Revenge is our religious duty. We beat the Russian superpower in Afghanistan; we can beat the Indian forces too. We fight with the help of Allah, and once we start jehad, no force can withstand us."

A budding Lashkar recruit in Muzaffarabad.

The young recruits of Lashkar, mostly slender college-aged Kashmiris with thin beards and solemn eyes, talked softly of unthinkable things. One described with pride how he had once hidden in a pine tree, pushing the button on a remote-control mine and watching excitedly as several Indian soldiers flew into the air. Another, who looked no more than sixteen, said his most fervent dream was to die in jehad against the Indians so he would secure a place in heaven. These boys had been plucked from poverty, taught to read the Koran and shoot a gun, and given a sense of deadly purpose. As I watched them and listened, I kept wondering how many of them would be dead within the year.

In Muzaffarabad, the political capital of Pakistani Kashmir that is home to thousands of exiles from across the border and the nexus of a system of training camps for insurgents, I learned too late that a mass funeral had just been held for six men who had been killed in combat at Kargil, their coffins borne through the city while pallbearers lofted their semiautomatic rifles and weeping residents shouted, "Holy war! Holy war!" But when I arrived the next afternoon, I visited a refugee camp where several of the dead combatants had lived; a cramped cauldron of political fervour where people spoke with deep bitterness of the oppression they had endured at the hands of Indian forces before fleeing from Indian Kashmir.

One gaunt old man, with a grey beard and piercing eyes, had just lost his twenty-two-year-old son in Kargil. But instead of mourning, he was blazing with righteous conviction as he described how he himself had once been tortured by Indian interrogators in Srinagar, how his eldest son had joined a rebel group and died in a shoot out with Indian forces several years ago, and how he now hoped he could offer his third and only remaining son to the cause. A group of teenagers listened in a circle around him, and someone carried the old man's grandson into the room. Pointing to the infant, he made a solemn pronouncement: "We are prepared to offer each of their lives for the glory of Islam and the liberation of Kashmir."

Just who were these men with soft voices and burning gazes? Were they creatures of a foreign conspiracy, taught only to kill and worship, manipulated by a foreign government and by pan-Islamic forces with religious and territorial designs on Kashmir — one of the most beautiful and strategically positioned regions of South Asia? Were they products of a generation of alienation and abuse at the hands of Indian authorities, and of deep-seated prejudice against Muslims by the Hindus of their homeland, driven to desperate acts after years of frustrated attempts at peaceful change? Or were they both?

To get closer to the truth, I realised I needed to spend some time in the Kashmir Valley itself, a haunted place where tens of thousands of people, including many of the region's best and brightest leaders, had already died in a decade of vicious guerilla war and military repression. My first impressions were of stark and incongruous contradictions. There were lush orchards and rice paddies, lakes covered with water lilies and breathtaking mountain vistas. But on every corner, unsmiling Indian soldiers were hunched in dank bunkers covered with anti-grenade nets, and on every major road, troops in camouflage uniforms patrolled day and night. In all my years of reporting abroad, covering insurgencies and riots and dictatorships, I had rarely felt such an intense and overwhelming military presence.

In a number of interviews, Indian Army and police and civilian officials painted a benign portrait of this presence, insisting that aside from a few aberrant excesses, the troops were a welcome source of protection for a terrorised populace in a region that had lost more than twenty thousand inhabitants (though the unofficial estimates are more than double) to political violence since 1989. They asserted that to a large extent, the local rebellion had been brought to its knees through years of counter-insurgency tactics, and was now reduced to a handful of foreign fighters operating under Pakistani direction. "There is no Kashmir problem," one police official told me serenely. "The only problem is Pakistan."

It took less than a week, however, to realise that India's military presence was a daily, deeply resented humiliation for many ordinary Kashmiris, and that a large number secretly supported the rebels. Jobless young men and elderly retirees, villagers and townspeople alike whispered the same, sullen comments about soldiers and the police who treated them like cattle, dragged off their sons or classmates for questioning, and took brutal, systematic revenge on places where militants were suspected to be hiding or active. If India dared to remove its troops for just one day, a middle-aged carpenter whispered, "then they would see what the people really think."

The animosity was especially palpable in areas where the Indian security forces had engaged in systematic and sometimes brutal counter-insurgency activities. One morning in early June, a Kashmiri journalist and I drove to a village called Khargam after hearing rumours that it had been burned to the ground. We arrived to find several hundred people milling in anguish amid the smouldering ruins of their home. Khargam was a carpet-weaving village, and strewn among the piles of rubble were charred looms, piles of singed wool and blackened shreds of elaborately decorated rugs. Each one had taken eight months to weave, we were told. In sheds beside the houses lay the charred bodies of still-tethered cows, their bellowing panic now mercifully silent.

The villagers all said the army and other security troops had come looking for two militants who were hiding nearby. They had herded all the inhabitants into several homes, cornered the militants and shot them. Then they doused the village with kerosene and

Pamela Constable

set it ablaze, refusing to let anyone return for their animals or belongings. The act was both punishment and warning. "They want to say to us, 'if you help the militants, we will do the same thing to each and every person, in each and every village'," said a local teacher. Instead, he said, "now each and every person has a new hatred in their heart."

The story I wrote about Khargam was instantly snatched up by Pakistani officials as proof of India's abusive role in Kashmir; they mentioned it in interviews and copied it for circulation. As a result, the story became somewhat controversial in India, where much of the press was flushed with patriotic fever and falling over itself to produce the next "brave jawan" story. One Delhi journalist asked me how I felt about having my reportage used as Pakistani propaganda during a war. My answer may have sounded disingenuous or callous, but it was true: once my work was in the public domain, it no longer belonged to me. If I started choosing whether and what to publish depending on whose ox it would gore, my credibility would instantly be gone.

In many ways, though, the story of Khargam was an old one in Kashmir: fanatical insurgents and ruthless government forces playing a violent game of cat and mouse, ordinary citizens caught in the middle, and an accurate account of what happened almost impossible to come by. In fact, the more I learned about the history of the Kashmiri militancy, the more it seemed to have been mired in contradictions, propaganda, rumours, half-truths, scapegoating, petty internal quarrels, competing versions of reality, and endlessly revised and debated political doctrine. Had there

(facing page) A girl sits on the window of her house in Khargam village, which was allegedly torched by the Indian Army.

been twenty thousand deaths, as the government claimed, or seventy thousand, as its opponents did? No death seemed to have been either simple or straightforward; every armed clash seemed to have a dozen explanations.

While there seemed to be widespread support for the home-grown militancy among ordinary Kashmiris, they expressed much more ambivalence towards the conflict in Kargil. Any connection between their long-standing struggle for self-determination and an invisible invasion along a remote stretch of border seemed tenuous. Many were wary of Pakistan's intentions after years of fruitless violence in the Valley, and although they were glad to see their cause suddenly gaining international attention, they also feared the Kargil conflict would attract foreign concern for the wrong reasons, namely fears that it could escalate into a nuclear conflagration.

Indeed, in early July, after years of keeping a careful and neutral distance from the Kashmir dispute, which it regularly insisted must be settled bilaterally between India and Pakistan, the United States intervened swiftly and unexpectedly to end the Kargil conflict. In Washington, President Clinton interrupted celebrations of the nation's Independence Day to hold a long private meeting with Pakistani prime minister Nawaz Sharif, and the two emerged from the White House to announce that Sharif would request the "freedom fighters" to withdraw from Indian territory for the sake of regional peace.

It appeared that Clinton had used both carrot and stick, threatening Sharif with further financial sanctions if the mountain-top occupation persisted but promising to take a "personal interest" in solving the long-standing Kashmir issue if Sharif pledged to de-escalate the growing military crisis with India. American officials, however, immediately downplayed any possibility of US intervention or mediation after India declared it unacceptable, and as the fighting in Kargil wound down, the Valley's troubles seemed likely to slip from world attention again.

"Instead of being an offshoot of Kashmir, Kargil itself became the issue. The aspirations of the Kashmiri people were forgotten," said Abdul Ghani Lone, a longtime Kashmiri opposition politician from the All Parties Hurriyat (Freedom) Conference. He noted wryly that despite years of international calls for peaceful dialogue on Kashmir, it was still "the poor little gun" that got the world's attention refocused on Kashmir. "India with its vast military might can crush the movement by force, but the cancer is still very much there," he insisted. "They keep taking forty buckets and forty more buckets of water out of the well, but the (poisoned) dog is still inside it. Until they get him out, the water will never be drinkable."

While many Kashmiris were clearly seething under Indian control, they seemed lost for a realistic alternative. They were not especially keen to become part of Pakistan, and prospects for a plebiscite on self-determination appeared extremely dim and far in the future. Opposition party leaders, asked about the future of Kashmir, began every answer with a tired mantra about the United Nations resolution of 1948. Many of them had clearly suffered a great deal for their cause; some had spent years in jail and lost their closest friends and relatives to violence. And yet there was a dream-like quality to their pronouncements; a blind commitment to an impossible ideal that had long been twisted beyond recognition by larger forces with agendas that had little to do with the rights of average Kashmiris.

Once the Kargil conflict had been called off, Islamic militant groups in Pakistan began warning they were going to create "new

Kargils" and revive their sabotage attacks in the Valley. And within days, they began to carry out their threat in earnest. During the second half of July and the first half of August, armed ambushes and rocket attacks exploded across Kashmir at a rate of nearly one every two days. More than fifty soldiers, security force members and civilians were killed in assaults on military posts and patrols from Bandipura to Kupwara, and the pace and ferocity of the attacks intensified as India's national elections approached in September.

Suddenly, the ghosts of Kashmir seemed to have been brought back to life. The militant movement that had virtually been declared dead by Indian authorities was exhibiting new muscle, firepower and ruthlessness. The tourist trade that had begun to revive in the spring, with Indian vacationers beginning to fill the long-vacant houseboats on Dal Lake and head into the glaciers on pony treks, had collapsed again. The armed forces, angry and embarrassed that the militants had rushed in to fill the void left by massive troop redeployments to Kargil, vowed to beef up their operations in the Valley.

As the deadly game of sabotage and retaliation started up again, ordinary Kashmiris seemed once again likely to suffer the consequences. While the rest of the country was preparing to vote under relatively peaceful conditions, Kashmir was once more becoming an armed camp, a place where campaigning was done under tight military scrutiny, candidates were harrassed, and many voters could anticipate only a sterile political exercise in which their dreams and fears remained unaddressed.

What lessons had been learned from the Kargil episode? Would greater military vigilance alone on India's part prevent another such incursion, or were Pakistan and the Muslim mujahideen groups prepared, as they vowed, to create "more Kargils" whenever possible? After so many years of fruitless bloodshed, was another era of violence about to begin again? Had the threat of a serious war between India and Pakistan, with the ominous corollary of nuclear conflagration now inevitably attached to it, brought either country closer to sitting down at the negotiating table — or had it only deepened their mutual suspicions and made the chance for diplomatic resolution that much more remote? What, indeed, was the solution to Kashmir's half-century of agony? A plebiscite? A permanent border? International mediation?

After two months of intensive reporting, the answers to such questions seemed more elusive to me than ever, and solutions that had seemed so simple and obvious at first now appeared hopelessly mired in the complex obstacles of history, geography, religion and politics. But I did gain some insights into why those obstacles existed, and especially into the sad irrelevance of both democratic processes and diplomatic efforts when a region and its people have become frozen in a tableau of violent extremes, almost unimaginable loss and suffering, and the perverse manipulation of symbiotic adversaries who have a vested interest in keeping the conflict alive. Finally, in Kargil and Kashmir, I relearned several lessons I had nearly forgotten in the four years since my last assignment overseas: war and death never get any easier to chronicle, and the "truth" about them is never totally what it seems.

'IT WAS NOT OUR WAR'

■ MUZAMIL JALEEL

> Most Kashmiris felt alienated from the Kargil war, though it was fought in their name. The war exposed both India and Pakistan in the Valley, says the Srinagar correspondent of *The Indian Express*.

'It Was Not Our War'

Eight persons, including a college student, a teacher and a butcher, are busy in a heated political discussion in a small barber shop in a narrow alley in downtown Srinagar. It is an early July afternoon. The place used to be the quiet domain of an old man who has been trimming hair and beards for decades. But ten years of violence in the region have turned it into a kind of sanctuary where people gather informally to vent their feelings in an atmosphere that is both familiar and safe.

This time the topic is nothing but Kargil. "Who are the people up there on the mountains?" someone asks. Not a single person present believes Pakistan's assertions that the fighters are Kashmiri militants, but some admit they are glad to see Indian troops on the defensive. "It is good, these people should know what a real war means. It is easy to stop civilian passenger buses and ask us to come down and frisk and humiliate even our womenfolk. Let them get a beating," says the college student, Firdous. The old barber shakes his head. "Never be happy with death, especially when you have seen so much here," he says, combing a client's beard serenely.

There is general agreement that the conflict in Kargil has at least meant fewer soldiers in Srinagar and in the villages of the Kashmir Valley — a welcome relief to all. "However, if it means the foreign militants will sneak into Srinagar, it's a worrying thought," the teacher, Shabir Ahmad, admits.

Warming to the subject of Kashmir history, he explains to the people around him how the Kargil war has exposed the weak military capability and ineffective strategy of Pakistan. "They should stop dreaming of Kashmir to be part of their country. And if they are our real friends, they should instead try to strengthen a movement for independent Kashmir," he says.

The men in the barber shop nod, finding some logic in his analysis. Encouraged, the teacher continues, "First, Pakistan doesn't have the guts to fight a war. It was a secret battle they didn't even acknowledge they were remotely involved in. Then they claimed that Islamic militant groups like Lashkar-e-Taiba and Harkat-ul-Mujahideen were up on the mountains. Why is it that only those who fight for Kashmir's merger with Pakistan on religious grounds are there? Why not those who are struggling for an independent Kashmir?"

An old man, who has been silent until now, speaks up. He is a retired revenue department employee, Abdul Rasheed. His voice has the authority of history lived as well as studied. "I have seen all the wars. You won't believe what a beating Pakistan received during the 1971 war. They had problems in East Pakistan because of the same policies India is employing in Kashmir, and they opened a front here also. The war was lost, and so was the spirit of Kashmiris. It was this defeat that paved the way for the Simla agreement, which turned Kashmir into a mere border dispute. And you will see, this Kargil misadventure is also set to break the back of resistance here," he observes.

For the first time during ten years of turmoil in Kashmir, he continues, "India has emerged on a stronger wicket internationally. This is the first time they have been able to have this image of being a victim. Everybody in the world seems to be for respecting this Line of Control by either side, though it is really nothing but a ceasefire line," he says.

Abdul Rasheed recalls being posted to Ladakh before the 1971 war, when Pakistani pickets were just across the Suru river in Kargil town. "The Pakistanis have made a mess of everything for us," he says bitterly. "They gave a part of Kashmir to China, and they kept one part which is nothing more than a colony of Islamabad. They think they can fool the world with this so-called Azaad Kashmir," he says with a snort, then falls silent again.

Suddenly a young man, Javeed, who is slumped in an empty barber's chair, cannot contain himself any longer. "I don't care who is up there on those mountains showering bullets and bombs on the Indian Army. I am happy after so many years," he bursts out. "Those across the borders are our brothers, they have the same faith as we have. And remember, we are being butchered in Kashmir not because we want to separate but because we are Muslims."

His anger, it turns out, has deep personal roots. His celebration of the Kargil invasion does not stem from any love of the infiltrators from across the border — but from hatred for the Indian security forces who killed his brother a few years ago. "How can we forget those who suffer for days while crossing the borders and then fight till martyrdom here? At least I can't forget my brother. They killed him in custody," he mumbles.

As the discussion becomes tense, the butcher, Ghulam Qadir, intervenes. He wonders whether a Kashmir Bandh, called by the All Parties Hurriyat Conference in support of the infiltrators fighting the Indian Army in Kargil, will be possible. "The hartals and strikes are once again back," Qadir comments worriedly. "Do you suppose there is any possibility of an intervention by America?"

It is an old refrain in Kashmir, a longtime dream that the US will come to the rescue and pressure India to negotiate. Like many others, those sitting here hope that the Kargil skirmish will help to internationalise Kashmir's dispute and lead to third-party mediation between the two hostile neighbours.

"I don't understand on what conditions Nawaz Sharif has agreed to withdraw," the barber says, frowning. "Is it just under international pressure or is there some truth in Clinton's assurance that he will do something within the next eighteen months?" According to the BBC, he adds, President Clinton has promised Sharif he will personally intervene.... Javeed, angry again, does not let the old man finish his sentence. "We should stop this wishful thinking," he says. "No outside power is going to help us ever. Have these Pakistanis forgotten that the promised Seventh Fleet never arrived to help them against India during the 1971 war?"

Once again, there is a need to defuse the tension in the shop. This time the old barber changes the topic. "Are you able to access Pak TV these days?" he asks blandly. "I heard there is a ban on it here." Qadir, the wise retiree, responds with some irritation: "There is nothing but Kargil on all these TV channels these days, both in India as well as across the border."

This comment draws a swift reaction. The school teacher says he was watching a programme about Kargil on Zee or Star and had then switched to Pak TV. "I was amazed to see the same feelings and fervour on both sides to not allow anybody to take Kashmir," he says. "Isn't it ironic — a soldier from Pakistani Gujarat or Punjab is fighting a soldier from Indian Gujarat or Punjab in the mountains of Kashmir. Have we turned into a battleground for these two countries who care more about the land than its inhabitants?"

It is getting late, so I leave the barber's shop. On my way back home, I encounter another discussion in the city bus. It has just stopped at the Kashmir University campus, so many of the passengers are young and opinionated. Once again, the topic is Kargil. Some professors are debating whether the participating troops will receive battle honours for the conflict, the first conventional military operations after a gap of twenty-eight years for both India and Pakistan. Someone else mentions how the counter-insurgents have joined the Indian Army as porters. Suddenly, an old man blurts out, "For Kashmiris, there are no Param Vir Chakras or Nishan-e-Haiders." Silence engulfs the entire bus. "We had reconciled with the accession to India, but look what they did to us. They broke their own promises. They never held the plebiscite, they jailed Sheikh Mohammad Abdullah and snatched our special status." His voice continues in an angry stream. "They ruled us through their corrupt agents, whose only qualification was that they were loyal to Delhi. They rigged elections and forced our youth to opt for guns," he says.

Now the old man turns his wrath on Pakistan. "What did those sitting across do to us? They placed guns in the immature hands of our youth. They trained our boys for a week or two, gave them a Kalashnikov rifle with a few hundred bullets and pushed them back to fight one of the world's largest armies. This war is not theirs. Their sons are not being butchered. They want to take revenge for the 1971 war and they are doing so through our youth." His rage finally exhausted, the old man falls silent.

I jump off the bus near the Tourist Reception Centre, thinking I will cross the Zero bridge on foot and reach my office. On my way, I meet two men. Both of them are in the tourism business, living on houseboats in Dal Lake. I can't help asking what the Kargil war has meant to them.

"This war has ruined us again. After ten years, our houseboats were once more full of tourists and we were expecting the old good days back. But Kargil finished it in two days. They all fled, cancelling their stay with us," says one of the men, Mohammad Ismail Dar. When the airport was closed after the war broke out, he recalls, there were more than fifty-five thousand tourists in Srinagar. "All the eleven hundred houseboats and dozens of hotels around Dal were full to their capacity. But within twenty-four hours the lake again wore that deserted look," he says disconsolately. Both the men are very angry that the war came at the height of the tourist season. "For us the fight for stomachs is more important than any other fight. Many a time during these past ten years, our children have had nothing to eat," the other man, Rafeeq, says bitterly.

As I reach my office, my head is filled with the echoes of all these confused and contradictory conversations. So many impassioned opinions, all of them based on a different personal or historical truth. So many problems, seemingly without answers. So many possible solutions, each with its own logic yet each with a series of reasons why it cannot work. The Kargil war, it seems, has once again brought out all the raging emotions, and exposed all the stubborn complexities, of the Kashmir problem. For me, it has strengthened my conviction that nonviolent means are the only way to resolve conflict. Kargil has proved another disaster for both India and Pakistan — even though India has declared "victory" and many people are ignoring the larger implications in the jingoism of nationalistic fervour on both sides. For fifty years the entire subcontinent tried and failed to overcome the animosity that grew out of Partition. Now, on the barren heights of Kargil, the seeds of regional hatred have been sown once more.

To most people of the Kashmir Valley, the Kargil war seemed a pale, distant and largely irrelevant echo of the terrible violence and suffering they had experienced during the past decade. From May to July, newspapers and TV channels were filled with emotional accounts of "brave jawans" killed or wounded on mountain tops, as several hundred bodies were brought home to grieving families amid a massive outpouring of national patriotic fervour. But Kashmiris felt so numb from the bloodshed that had taken thousands of lives in the Valley since 1989, and so alienated from the invisible border conflict only a hundred miles away, that they barely reacted at all — even though the fighting was entirely in the name of Kashmir.

'It Was Not Our War'

"It was not our war," Mohammad Yousuf, an old shopkeeper in Dalgate, told me one day in July, as a huge convoy of army trucks and Bofors gun batteries returning from Kargil passed by. The jawans were happy and waving to the crowds on the boulevard road in Srinagar, but there was virtually no reciprocation. The few men and women who did wave towards the armymen were tourists from Mumbai. "We are sick of wars and violence," Yousuf said. "We know what bombs and bullets do. Perhaps that is why we don't want that. We have been witnessing it for more than a decade now."

Across India, it seemed, everyone was caught up in the euphoria of the war — blood donation camps for soldiers fighting in Kargil, newspapers full of fundraising advertisements to aid the families of those who laid down their lives in Kargil, etc. But in Kashmir, there was nothing. Even for the Kashmiri armymen who died in the fighting, there were no emotional scenes at funeral processions. There was no one to cry and wail for them except their family members and relatives. Even friends hesitated to exhibit their grief. And, ironically, they were not even buried in the "martyrs' graveyard" set up in almost every village for those who died fighting Indian security forces or were caught in crossfire.

But the reaction to the Kargil conflict among Kashmiris also changed as the weeks passed. First there was a feeling of righteous satisfaction, because India had been caught off guard and was suffering battlefield casualties. Gradually, however, public sentiment turned to anger towards Pakistan, because people felt betrayed when the government in Islamabad agreed to pull out. In doing so, they reasoned, Pakistan had legitimised the Indian hold on Kashmir.

There was a more immediate reason why Kashmiris initially welcomed the invisible war in the distant mountain tops of Kargil: the conflict brought temporary relief to a region that had been bowed under the heavy presence of Indian troops for years. Redeploying many of these troops to Kargil meant less crackdown operations, less checkpoints and less army movement in many villages and towns. "I am happy not to be questioned by the troops so frequently now. Three army camps have been vacated in our area and the troops sent to the battle front," said Ghulam Mohammad Dar, a farmer from Safapora I met on the bus from Srinagar to Bandipura. "The Kargil war has simply eased our lives." The director-general of police in Jammu & Kashmir, Gurbachan Jaggat, also admitted that the Kargil war had weakened the overall security grid in the Valley. In fact, the army was pulled out of counter-insurgency operations and the responsibility entrusted to the Rashtriya Rifles, a paramilitary force. The directorate of that force was also shifted to Srinagar.

Although the problems of Kashmiris in Srinagar get more attention because of the city's political prominence, people in the rural areas have often had to bear the harshest brunt of the ongoing conflict between the army and the militants. Human rights abuses have been constant but rarely reported. In several Handawar and Kupwara villages, the villagers have been forced to patrol throughout the night alongside Indian troops, who use them as human shields in case of a militant attack. There are shifts for every family. In the early mornings, village men are known to have been ordered to walk ahead of security patrols meant to clear the roads of land mines and explosive devices.

Ironically, the militants do not treat the villagers much better either. They may barge into any house at gunpoint and stay for twenty-four hours, requiring the family to feed them and refusing

'It Was Not Our War'

After years of living in the crossfire of a political struggle, many Kashmiris took grim pleasure in the growing Indo-Pak tension.

to allow anyone to go out. If the security forces are tipped off to their presence, the troops inevitably arrive and launch an assault that blasts the house to bits and leaves the family shelterless. Moreover, the government has a policy of denying all relief for such families — it refuses to acknowledge that their collaboration with the militants may not have been voluntary.

After years of enduring the humiliation, hardship and constant anxiety of living in the crossfire of a violent political struggle, many Kashmiris from rural areas of the Valley took a kind of grim pleasure in the growing tensions between India and Pakistan. "There should be a full-fledged war now, to finish this matter once and for all. How long will we suffer in this situation, which is neither war nor peace?" demanded Mohammad Abdullah, a farmer from the village of Lolab. Forced to abandon his village, his land

and his cherished orchid nursery after life in the countryside became too treacherous, Abdullah now lives a hand-to-mouth life in Srinagar, crammed into two rented rooms with his family of six. "Douh diesh marni khouti chou behtar ikewatta mareun" (It is better to die once and for all than suffer a daily death), he said.

To a certain extent, exposure to the suffering of Indian troops in the Kargil conflict softened the attitudes of some Kashmiris towards the forces they had come to identify exclusively with oppression and abuse. As TV channels started airing the funerals of soldiers with interviews of their families, some Kashmiris, especially women, began relating to it. The death of a MiG pilot, Flight Lt. Ajay Ahuja, was a noticeable turning point. One night in late May, shortly after his plane had been shot down just inside Pakistan, I went to a neighbour's house in Srinagar. The room was full and the family was watching the evening bulletin on TV. As Ahuja's four-year-old son lit his funeral pyre, I realised the women were all in tears. One old lady, who had always cursed the army, was weeping at the death of an Indian soldier. I could not resist and asked her why. "Son, I know what it means to lose a young son, what it means to get orphaned," she said. The family's eldest son had been killed when the security forces mistook the sound of a tyre bursting for a militant attack and fired indiscriminately.

There was, however, little doubt among people in the Valley that the fighters in the peaks of Kargil were not freedom fighters interested in the cause of Kashmir, but a combination of Pakistani soldiers and militants from across the border. In fact, nobody believed the Pakistani rhetoric that local Kashmiri elements were up there. There were several reasons for this belief. If any local militant had indeed been killed in the fighting, the news would certainly have reached his family — and there had been no such information. In fact, the Jammu & Kashmir Liberation Front (JKLF), the only indigenous group in Kashmir which has no non-Kashmiri members, denied outright that it participated in the Kargil war. Only the pan-Islamic Lashkar-e-Taiba and Harkat-ul-Ansar — both controlled by non-Kashmiris — issued statements in Pakistan claiming that they had sent their men up. The two groups, predominantly non-Kashmiri, have in their ranks militants from Pakistan, Afghanistan, Algeria, Chechenya, Somalia and other Islamic countries. The Hizbul Mujahideen, another pro-Pakistan Islamic outfit, also claimed to have fought on the peaks but there was no news of any of their men being killed there.

As the weeks passed and the tables started turning in Kargil, Kashmiris began showing their anger against Pakistan. "If they knew they had to withdraw, why did they launch this misadventure in the first place?" demanded Ghulam Nabi Bhat, a college teacher from Baramulla. After the failure at Kargil, he expressed skepticism about the possibility of another military adventure by Pakistan to "liberate" Kashmir. "The results of the Kargil conflict, especially the way the international community reacted to it, has left no doubt that it will never support any such adventure launched by either side," he said.

At times, the feelings of Kashmiris resembled the post-1971 war period, when most had lost faith in Pakistan's ability to take Kashmir by violent means. "This war has strengthened our belief that only an indigenous political movement for an independent Kashmir will force both the countries to leave us alone," a pro-independence activist, Ashraf, told me. "We have no doubts that any more incursions of this type will have nothing to do with us. Isn't it ironic? It is they who fight for our land, decide to solve the issue bilaterally, and then decide to become 'bus' friends. Later, they go to war again and never bother to involve us, when it is our fate being decided. Nothing will help to resolve the Kashmir issue unless the people of Kashmir are accepted as a party," he said.

Although the common view heard in the streets of Kashmir by mid-July was that Pakistan had been defeated in Kargil, there were some who insisted that the intrusion was not a debacle for Pakistan after all. In the first place, India's victory came at a high cost of life and money, threatening to weaken its strength and cohesion in the long run, as had happened in the erstwhile Soviet Union. Second, it allowed for a rejuvenation of the floundering militancy movement in Kashmir, both by physically permitting people to cross over the LoC and by psychologically rekindling the lost morale among Kashmiris at a time when the majority of active militants here are foreigners. Third, it enabled Pakistan to successfully test the hypothesis that in a post-nuclear subcontinent, India would not risk a full-fledged war and Pakistan could get away with any adventure.

One Kashmiri who believed Pakistan gained something from the conflict was Tahir Mohideen, a columnist and editor of the Urdu weekly, *Chattan*. "How can one ignore the economic repercussions of holding the peaks in Kargil?" he demanded, noting that India's daily expenditure there was going to be in several crores of rupees. "Until now," he added, "Kashmir had always been paramount and India was willing to bear any cost to keep it. This is the first time any opinion has been raised questioning this, the first time that the huge burden on the exchequer is being questioned."

A disturbing fallout of the Kargil war is the spurt in violence and the alarming rise in infiltration of militants in Kashmir. As Mohideen pointed out: "More than seventy per cent of the militancy had been crushed in the state, especially in the Kashmir Valley, and there were no indications of a revival. But since the Kargil war started, the situation has come back to square one." Mohideen estimated that enough militants (about fifteen hundred) had now sneaked into the Valley and the border districts of Jammu to easily sustain militancy for the next five years. "This was possible only because of the void created in the security situation during Kargil," he said. Mentioning the daredevil attacks by the militants on army camps in Kupwara in August, he said it was an especially dangerous development: the first time during a decade of separatist violence that the militants had dared to openly attack army establishments.

The government too is worried: the minister of state for home in the Jammu & Kashmir government, Mushtaq Ahmad Lone, claimed that the introduction of suicide squads in the militant ranks was a fallout of the Kargil war. "After the withdrawal from the Kargil heights, these foreign militants have been diverted to Kupwara and other border districts," he said.

These suicide squads, called "Fidayeen," are apparently part of all militant outfits now. They do not use cyanide pills to commit suicide like the LTTE of Sri Lanka. But they are a bunch of highly dedicated and motivated religious fanatics — they have come into Kashmir not for love of money but for jehad. According to Gurbachan Jaggat, the director general of Jammu & Kashmir police, "They basically take on dangerous missions, like entering into an army camp, where they believe there are minimal chances of returning alive." The "Fidayeen" are a post-Kargil phenomenon, and the security agencies in Kashmir believe there is every likelihood that the same men, along with Pakistani regulars, were up on the icy peaks in Kargil — an operation that was no less suicidal in nature.

There is a minority view that though Pakistan failed on the diplomatic front, its main goal to internationalise the Kashmir issue was achieved. "It is true that instead of coming up as an offshoot of the Kashmir dispute, Kargil became an issue in itself," said Mohideen. "But India could not isolate it either. The international community restricted itself to diffusing the tensions to prevent a full-fledged war, but it also meant that the root cause of Indo-Pak hostility — the Kashmir issue — was being discussed in every forum." If nothing else, he concluded with some hopefulness, "at least the world will now stress the need for greater autonomy to both sides of Kashmir."

For Kashmiris associated with the "separatist, independent Kashmir" ideology, the Kargil conflict trapped them in a catch-22 dilemma. They could not support India, as a matter of conviction and tradition, but they also could not take a strong anti-Pakistan line, because they were not "in a position to open up another front" and start an insurgency against Pakistan. In 1992, the JKLF — the largest group professing a separatist view —had organised a peaceful march across the LoC from Pakistan-occupied Kashmir (PoK) to show that they did not recognise the division of the state. Pakistan used massive force to stop this march, shooting at least ten participants dead. The reason, many pro-independence Kashmiris believe, was that Pakistan does not want a "third option" for Kashmir — that of independence. "Our struggle is not acceptable to either country. If India kills us here, Pakistan's attitude is no different," a senior JKLF leader told me in Srinagar. "They stopped our activists from crossing over in exactly the same way the Indian administration does."

Yaseen Malik, the thirty-three-year-old chief of the JKLF, stated flatly that there was no one from his organisation fighting on the Kargil peaks. "We have proclaimed a cease-fire in 1994, and since then all our military activities against India have come to a halt, even though more than five hundred of our men have been killed here during this period," he said. He strongly denied charges that his movement for an independent Kashmir was "Muslim fundamentalist" or affiliated with militant Islamic groups such as Lashkar-e-Taiba and Harkat-ul-Ansar, which claimed they had taken a front seat in the Kargil fighting. "Lashkar is not the voice of Kashmiri people," Malik insisted. "Kashmiris want freedom from both India and Pakistan. Our aim is an independent Kashmir."

Sitting in a small dingy room at his modest residence in Srinagar, Malik puffed on cigarette after cigarette as he spoke passionately of the Kargil war. "We have been turned into cannon fodder between two hostile neighbours," he said angrily. Kashmir, he said, has never been just a bilateral issue between India and Pakistan. "It is not a cattle herd that they have to divide. It is the fate of human beings, the fate of more than twelve million people who live across the state," he said.

Malik's views on Kargil were grounded in a careful, if partisan, analysis of the region's fifty-year history since the Partition of the Indian subcontinent. Since 1947, he said, various issues emerged as a direct fallout of the dispute over Kashmir — from local incidents such as the 1993 theft of the holy relic from Hazratbal shrine in Srinagar, to events with international implications such as the three wars between the two neighbours and their deciding to conduct nuclear tests in 1998. Now, he added, there was going to be a "fallout" of the Kargil conflict — this time with new and more dangerous implications for regional peace.

"This war has vindicated our point," Malik said. "We have always warned the international community to intervene and pressure both India and Pakistan to resolve the Kashmir dispute in accordance with the aspirations of the people." "Otherwise," he added darkly, "they better remain ready for some massive destruction." Now that Kargil has opened the world's eyes, Malik said, they must remain open until the problem of Kashmir is solved, or such incidents of "fallout" will continue.

There was some disagreement among other separatist leaders in Kashmir about whether the Kargil conflict had helped or hurt their cause. Syed Ali Shah Geelani, the seventy-year-old leader of the All Parties Hurriyat Conference (APHC) — an agglomeration of mostly pro-Pakistan separatist groups — said it had strengthened the group's long-standing demand for a peaceful resolution of Kashmir dispute. But Geelani, a veteran leader of the pro-Pakistan Jamaat-e-Islami party, felt strongly that Pakistan should not have withdrawn the mujahideen from Kargil, and that it should have consulted the APHC before doing so.

Geelani objected strongly to the continuous Pakistani shelling of towns and villages in the Kargil area, calling it an "inhuman action." But he did not object to militants sneaking into Kargil from Pakistan, arguing that it was no crime to cross a border that "is not acceptable to us." More broadly, Geelani said he did not see anything wrong with the presence of foreign militants in the struggle against India. "Whenever any nation is fighting a moral and just cause, the whole civilised world comes to their support," he said, noting that India had justified its intervention in East Pakistan in 1971 on grounds that it was fighting the suppression of the populace. "Why does this argument not hold true for Kashmir?"

In contrast, another longtime separatist leader, Shabir Shah, said he believed there was no justification for war between India and Pakistan, largely because Kashmiris inevitably suffer the worst consequences of such hostilities. "War will never help resolve issues," he said, praising the Sharif-Clinton meeting for

'It Was Not Our War'

Separatist Shabir Shah (in white, centre) believes that war is futile as the Kashmiris will inevitably suffer the consequences.

stopping the Kargil conflict before it escalated seriously. He also said he was especially concerned about the inhabitants of Kargil, who were at the receiving end during this conflict. "No one cares for them," he protested. "Their homes are being shelled and they are not even allowed to move to safer places. War always has its implications for the common man," he said. "Think how much money both countries wasted on those uninhabited peaks — and it all came from the pockets of the poor."

Though the fallout of the Kargil conflict was generally negative in Kashmir, it was positive on one sector of the political scene: the pro-India political camps. Their feeling is that the Kargil defeat may demoralise pro-Pakistan elements in Kashmir and lead to a situation where "disenchanted and misled" youth will start getting disillusioned with Pakistan. More broadly, Kargil galvanised the pre-election political scene in Kashmir. Most mainstream parties have long sought a political package from the Central government that would restore greater autonomy to the state. Once this was a popular slogan of the National Conference alone, but suddenly all major political parties in Kashmir are demanding it. In fact, Mufti Mohammad Sayeed, a veteran pro-India politician in Kashmir, and his daughter, Mehbooba Mufti, who broke off from the Congress this summer and launched a new party, the People's Democratic Party, changed their long time pro-centrist politics with a pro-autonomy manifesto.

The National Conference leadership has also begun to talk about the implementation of the State Autonomy Report that was released by the state government a few months ago. "In the backdrop of the Kargil victory, the Centre should immediately take measures at the domestic level so that the tremendous international support can be sustained. And restoration of autonomy is the only way," a senior National Conference leader said. The other opinion gaining currency is that since Pakistan has betrayed the spirit of the Lahore Declaration by invading Kargil, nothing can ever be achieved by talking to Islamabad; therefore, why not talk to the militants? Mufti's party strongly recommends an unconditional dialogue between the Centre, the militants and their representative bodies, such as the APHC.

Mehbooba Mufti, an articulate and impressive young politician, said her party's stand had been vindicated by the Kargil war. "Kargil has again proven that Kashmir is a flash point and that there is an immediate need to resolve this dispute across the table," she said. "Whenever there is an increase in the hostilities between these two neighbours, there is havoc in Kashmir." As war was raging in the Kargil heights, she said, the security forces let loose a reign of terror in Kashmir and more than 150 residential houses, comprising two full villages, were burned to the ground.

Mufti said she was disturbed by what she called a double standard in the response of many Indians towards the Kargil war and the bloodshed in Kashmir. "Those few hundred men who died in the Kargil war were our brothers. But look at the euphoria that this war generated," she said. "The whole country was united in helping the survivors of those who were killed on the Kargil peaks — sacrificed for the sake of barren mountains and rocks. But here in Kashmir, twenty deaths daily have been a routine for the past ten years now and nobody ever cared. When they say, 'Kashmir to Kanyakumari is one,' is that a mere slogan? Aren't human beings dying in Kashmir too?"

The Bharatiya Janata Party (BJP) wields almost no influence in Kashmir, but while the Kargil "victory" was a mainstay of the party's election campaign nationwide, its local leaders expressed a pragmatic and not unsympathetic understanding of the Kashmiris' indifference to the conflict and its outcome. "Kashmiris did not attach as much importance to this issue as people did in the rest of the country," said Abdul Rasheed Kabli, the party's Kashmir leader. Local BJP activists were not engulfed in nationalistic fervour, he claimed, adding that they would like to see relations with Pakistan move in the direction of the Lahore Declaration — not in the direction of Kargil. "Both India and Pakistan are now nuclear powers. If these nukes were ever used, Kashmir would be the first target," he said. "We are being directly hit by the war, so we want peace."

Ironically, one of the most gung-ho Kashmiris on the subject of Kargil is a former militant, Mohammad Yousuf (alias Kukka)

Parrey, who once headed an insurgent group called Ikhwan-ul-Muslimoon, but who surrendered with his group in the mid-1990s and later launched a massive counter-insurgency campaign in north Kashmir. Then he launched a political outfit, the Awami League, ran for an assembly seat and was elected from Sonawari. This summer, Parrey claimed to have sent sixty-five of his boys to help the Indian Army as voluntary porters and guides in Kargil.

"I organised a huge gathering in Hajin village to show our solidarity with the troops fighting up there," Parrey told me. "My boys were ready even to cross the LoC, but the army commanders asked us to look after the heights in Safapora and Bandipura, as the troops had been mobilised to Kargil." Parrey said he was proud of his group's sacrifice for the country's security, but also felt somewhat bitter. "I have lost more than five hundred of my men during the past few years of war with militants in Kashmir, including my two nephews," he said. "One of my commanders died fighting militants who killed five members of his family. There was no recognition of these sacrifices. There was no gallantry award for any of my men," as there were for the heroes of Kargil, he said. "But it doesn't bother me. We did our job well."

It was yet another addition to the graveyard in the south Kashmir village of Dachnipara. Another young man, Abdul Salam Dar, had been killed at the age of twenty-one, leaving behind his elderly mother, two sisters and two brothers. For years, villages in south Kashmir had given sleepless nights to the Indian security forces. They were said to be the bastions of certain hardcore militants, who had wreaked havoc on local military posts and patrols. Dozens of men had died violent deaths there in recent years; how many had died in the past decade was impossible to count. But all were young, most of them were idealistic, and had

'It Was Not Our War'

The body of a Kashmiri soldier in the Indian Army killed in Kargil being brought back to his village.

believed they were fighting for something that mattered.

This time, however, a boy from Dachnipara died for entirely different reasons, under entirely different circumstances. Abdul Salam Dar was an armyman of 12 Jammu and Kashmir Light Infantry. He was killed in action on the ridges of Batalik, fighting infiltrators who were predominantly regular Pakistani troops. Dar was the first boy from this entire area to join the army in 1994, when militancy was at its peak. He was probably the only man from this area to die fighting the Pakistanis.

Two men from a village in Shathpora in Kupwara district — Dost Mohammad Khan and Nazil Ahmad — were also killed fighting for India in Kargil, but they belonged to traditional army families — their village had sent men to join the army since the

1940s. "We fight as it is our duty after we join the army and take the oath. Dying in action is also part of our duty," said Dilawar Khan, the father of Mohammad.

But what did the Kargil war mean to Dar's family and village, a place and people who had known little but the abusive side of Indian military might? And what was the response of the people and the government to his sacrifice? These were the first questions that struck me the moment I entered the two-storey mud house in this remote hamlet. The family was still in shock. No one at home could read or write, so someone sent for a better educated cousin to talk to me and my colleague. In fact, Dar had been the only educated child in the family.

The cousin, Mohammad Tahir, arrived and started speaking. At first, I felt as if he had worked out a politically correct story, describing Dar's bravery and devotion to duty. I sensed the same distrust of strangers in him that so many Kashmiris have adopted as a survival technique in a maelstrom of violence, propaganda and betrayals. But after a few moments, he realised I was a fellow Kashmiri who spoke his language and understood his family's dilemma. With that, he started pouring his heart out. He said Dar had joined the army because getting any other job was impossible. He said there were more than a hundred boys and girls of the village who had no work. Then Dar's elder brother, Gul Mohammad, spoke up. "He was brave and he laid his life for the Qasam (oath) parade," he said.

Dar's family said they hated Pakistan. But had they started loving India after they lost a son fighting for this country? The answer was clearly no. "As our brother was braving the Pakistani bullets on the icy peaks in Batalik, I was ruthlessly beaten up by the Special Operation Group without any reason here outside my house," said Gul Mohammad. And although the family believes

'It Was Not Our War'

Dar died a martyr's death, there are many in the village who disagree. In the first few days of Dar's death, they said, the whole village showed sympathy. But as the days passed, things started changing. "Nobody says it, but you know how people think about the army here," said Tahir.

Dar's sister, who also joined us, said the family had no interest in the war or the politics behind it. "Our brother was in the army, and he was the sole source of income for the whole family. We just know one thing, we have nobody now," she said. Dar's mother, Jana Bano, is in her eighties. Broken by his death, she said the world was already finished for her.

The patriotic outpouring of sentiment for India's Kargil martyrs so evident throughout the rest of India, was glaringly absent in Dachnipara. There were no condolences published in the local newspapers. There were no donations for Dar's survivors. In fact, according to the family, no state government minister visited the family to condole the death.

Tahir, asked by Dar's brothers to seek help on their behalf, said he felt completely helpless, and that nobody in the government had helped him complete the formalities to apply for relief and benefits. "I had gone to meet the deputy commissioner of Anantnag in this connection," he said. "I had to wait three hours until I got permission to enter his office. There is no honour for Kargil martyrs here, even in our government."

Unlike the people of Kashmir, the Kargilis were direct victims of the border conflict. Pakistani shells struck their houses and fields regularly, sometimes killing people and animals. Thousands of families were forced to migrate from their ancestral homes, leaving everything behind. Although most Kargilis are Muslims, they have generally taken a pro-India stance, and perhaps this explained why they were targeted so heavily from across the LoC. In Kargil, continuous shelling from Pakistani artillery had become a fact of life since 1997. But now, with Indian troops fighting in the nearby peaks, the bombardment intensified even more.

The most immediate effect of the war was one of massive dislocation. More than twenty thousand people from at least twenty villages from north of Kargil town fled to areas miles away for safety. They were evacuated in army trucks, but there were no special arrangements for them, no camps or government assistance. Most took shelter in the homes of local families in villages such as Mingee and Trespone, sharing their food and meagre space. In many cases, this meant as many as ten people sleeping in one room.

One family, after weeks of frustration and idleness as refugees, decided to return to their village on the banks of the Suru river, thinking the war had subsided. One of their sons, Mohammad Musa, went out to offer morning prayers. As he was returning home, a Pakistani shell landed and killed him instantly. At his funeral, his mother wailed in consternation, asking over and over, "Why do they fire at us? What have we ever done to them?"

In the town of Kargil, a number of shells struck the local hospital, forcing the staff to shift the operating rooms and several other essential departments outside town. The doctors also reported that as a result of heavy shelling, many people sought treatment for shattered nerves and insomnia, and they observed an alarming increase in the number of premature deliveries and post-traumatic stress disorder.

Schools were also targeted for shelling, so most had to be closed. Some enterprising teachers in private schools opened temporary classrooms in tents, but they were hampered by a lack of books and other supplies, and they found it difficult to reassure,

'It Was Not Our War'

Anxious refugees from Kargil wait for supplies in Mingee.

educate and entertain young children who had left behind their homes, their playmates and their familiar surroundings.

"These children are not able to understand what happened to make them leave the comfort of their homes and share a room at a relative's house miles away," said Ghulam Ali, a teacher who was holding classes in a tent in Tresone. I asked one little boy there what the war had meant to him, and he answered, "It is going far away from home, and having my sisters stay in a different house."

Those civilians who decided to remain behind and face the shells rather than seek refuge elsewhere ended up spending most of their time in poorly constructed, inadequate underground bunkers, about a thousand of which had been built by the state government. They were far from fit to live in, and nobody believed they were safe either. "If a stone is thrown on their roofs, they will come down, not to speak of a shell," Bakir Ali, a shopkeeper in Kargil, told me. Even Qamar Ali Akhoon, a local politician from the National Conference who represents Kargil in the state legislature and who spent the war camping in Kargil, admitted that the bunkers were neither secure nor habitable.

As a result of their privations, the people of Kargil were extremely angry with Pakistan for invading the heights and destroying their peaceful existence. "I don't understand why they occupied these barren mountains. What will they achieve by doing so?" asked a student, Maqsood Hussain. "If they claim that India has forcibly occupied Kargil against the wishes of its Muslim inhabitants, then why are they targeting us?"

And yet many people in Kargil also harboured strong feelings of resentment against India as well. Their indignation rose higher after a senior army commander as also the state's chief minister, Farooq Abdullah, charged that there were Pakistani "moles" or agents in Kargil, spying for Pakistani fighters and helping them guide their artillery fire to certain targets. Police officials in Kargil town also said they were concerned about this problem, and that searching for such agents was their top priority during the period of intense conflict.

"Who would direct artillery fire on his own house and get his children killed?" protested Asgar Ali Karbalai, general secretary of a local Shia non-profit organisation, the Imam Khomeini Memorial Trust. The group has close ties to Iran, as do many members of Kargil's Shia Muslim community, but Karbalai insisted none of them would abet Pakistan. If any Kargilis had acted as agents for the Pakistani Army, he asserted, "the shells would have generally hit military areas, not civilian ones."

Karbalai also demanded to know how so many infiltrators had managed to come so close to Kargil and the Srinagar-Leh national highway, despite the presence of tens of thousands of Indian troops on the border. "They did not cross the LoC in a day. They did not construct cement bunkers in a week," he said sarcastically. Both Karbalai and Akhoon were equally upset at the accusations of spying for Pakistan. Karbalai called such charges "an insult to

Kargilis resent accusations of spying for Pakistan and point out that they have in fact been cooperating with the Indian Army since 1947.

the people of Kargil. If we had not wanted the Indian Army here, the troops would never have been able to stay even a single day." Kargil was the only Muslim-dominated area of Kashmir, he pointed out, where militancy had not been able to strike roots. "We have been providing guides and porters to the army since 1947, and now look what we get in return."

Further, Akhoon claimed that the army had been informed last year by the locals that there was a threat of cross-border incursions in Batalik, but the officials paid no attention. "If they don't do their work well, what can we do?" he shrugged. "There is not a single inhabited area around these peaks, and it is all controlled by the army. What have we to do with it?"

Even after the fighters from Pakistan withdrew and the pace of shelling diminished, Akhoon said he was concerned about what would happen to his Kargili constituents during the coming winter, when the snow would make the mountain passes along the highway impossible to cross. "We generally stock our food, firewood and other things during the summer, because in winter we are cut off for six months from the outside world," he said. "This year we could do nothing. Even those who were out of the shelling zone had to share everything they had with the migrants. So they too are in trouble."

Akhoon complained that there had been a pattern of official discrimination against Kargilis who sought to join the Indian armed forces. For years, he said, he has requested in vain that the army form a unit of Kargil Scouts, based on the model of the highly regarded Ladakh Scouts. "Our boys are being used by the army as porters and guides. Why can't they be armymen and defend the borders on these peaks themselves?" he demanded. His petition was not only a plea for justice, it was also based on common sense. "A soldier from the plains of Bihar or Punjab finds it very difficult here, but our boys have grown up here," Akhoon said. "This high-altitude life is in our blood."

Although the fighting in the hills of Kargil was as invisible to the local civilian population as it was to other, more distant inhabitants of the region, the people of Kargil bore the worst and most direct brunt of the border conflict. Pakistan shelled their homes and drove them off their lands. India failed to provide shelter for them and ignored warnings of the coming invasion.

Sometimes, it seemed to these Kargilis, the discrimination was such that even animals in Leh received better treatment from the authorities than people from Kargil. According to another member of the Khomeini Trust, when the snow came early to Leh one year and some herds of goats were facing starvation, the government airdropped supplies of grass. But this summer, when people in Kargil were being shelled, "nobody bothered," he said bitterly. "The government should realise that Kargil does not mean Tololing and Tiger Hill alone. There are also human beings living here."

The Kargil war was fought, won and lost. Both India and Pakistan claimed victory, amid jingoism and nationalistic fervour. But in Kashmir, both sides seem to have lost. The war on the barren mountains of Kargil has exposed both India and Pakistan in the Valley. For those Kashmiris who believed in "Kashmir to Kanyakumari is one," many queries arise. Why was this sympathy wave missing when Kashmiris were being killed for the past ten years? Why was there no newspaper advertisement to collect donations for victims of violence in Kashmir? Why was there no outpouring of nationalistic fervour even when fifty civilians were killed on a Srinagar street?

And if people outside the Valley felt many Kashmiris were hostile to India, why was there no such public outcry when Kashmiris died in the name of India or the militants committed massacres like the killings of twenty-three Kashmiri pandits (Hindus), including an infant? Why did nobody across the country bother when entire families were wiped out by either side? Indeed, for Kashmiris who believe that India is not their country, its extraordinary emotional investment in Kargil seemed to vindicate their conviction that in their heart of hearts, many Indians do not view Kashmiris as members of their nation.

Pakistan, on the other hand, exposed its lust for the majestic and beautiful land of Kashmir. April and May had been a happy interlude for Kashmir. For the first time in ten years the tourism trade, the backbone of its economy, was booming again. But with the eruption of war along the border, this happy hiatus ended abruptly. In theory, Pakistan and its "freedom fighters" invaded Kargil in the name of liberating Kashmir — yet they never took their Kashmiri beneficiaries into confidence, not even the APHC, which Pakistan acknowledges as the sole valid political organisation there.

Both India and Pakistan, it seemed, were far more interested in their own geographic, religious and military agendas than they were in the suffering inhabitants of Kashmir. After ten weeks of costly military conflict, Kashmir was left exactly as it had been before: humiliated by daily military harrassment, afflicted by a new outburst of militant attacks, and silently clinging to a dream of freedom that seemed as distant as ever.

In The 'Enemy Country'

■ BHARAT BHUSHAN

> The executive editor of *The Hindustan Times*, who was in Pakistan during the Kargil conflict, finds the civil and military elite there admitting that the intrusion was a miscalculation. He also finds many extremist, anti-India voices in Pakistan.

In the 'Enemy Country'

The air is remarkably clean in Islamabad, the temperature is moderate, the bougainvillaea is in full bloom and since this is the monsoon season so is sawani flowering with its pink, purple and white flowers along broad road dividers. Islamabad is a marvellously planned city at the foot of the beautiful Margalla hills. To get a panoramic view of its broad tree-lined avenues and grand government buildings, one has to drive up to Daman-i-Koh on top of the Margalla hills. On a clear day, one can even see Kahuta from there.

The serpentine drive to the top of the Margalla hills, I know, will have to wait. There is work at hand immediately as there is a Lashkar-e-Taiba rally in Aabpara, which should be quite interesting to attend. It is the first Lashkar rally — or for that matter any political rally — in Islamabad after the Pakistani decision to withdraw from Kargil. Only a day earlier, Lashkar-e-Taiba had organised a highly successful protest rally against Prime Minister Nawaz Sharif's decision to withdraw from Kargil at Lahore's Mochi Gate. Everyone is curious to know how successful the rally in Islamabad will be.

The main dais has been set up quite audaciously right in the middle of Khyaban-e-Suhrawardy where it crosses Municipal Road G-6 at Aabpara Market. The road has been blocked and chairs are in place for a couple of thousand people. On both sides of the road are four to five feet high models of Ghauri and Shaheen missiles.

Incidentally, Nawaz Sharif has given Pakistan two new national symbols which seek to define its identity — Chagai hills, where the nuclear tests of May 1998 were conducted, and the Ghauri missile. Ugly replicas of both at which Pakistani taxi drivers never forget to point have been constructed at a considerable cost to the national exchequer, at major roundabouts in all cities. Lashkar-e-Taiba has gone a step further and carries to its rallies scaled-down models of Ghauri and Shaheen missiles as symbols of Pakistani manhood.

What is remarkable about the rally is that the security arrangements are totally in the hands of a rag-tag group of the armed activists or the so-called mujahideen from the Lashkar. They move around with confidence, telling people what to do but more importantly, what not to do. They tell journalists sitting outside Kamran Restaurant at the venue of the meeting not to smoke or take any pictures. A mujahideen wearing a black shawl with Lashkar-e-Taiba printed on it stands guard over the rally on top of a pillar in the courtyard of the restaurant advertising Cornetto ice cream.

The so-called mujahideen are easily distinguishable from the rest of the crowd by their sunburnt faces, long beards, their unkempt hair peeping out of their Afghan chakrali caps and their battle fatigues stitched as Pathani suits worn often with rubber slippers or thin canvas shoes. Those who don't have guns — and not all of them do — walk around with thick wooden sticks. The local police are clearly merely marking their presence.

A banner at the rally proclaims that "Jehad (holy war) is a road which if followed can bring you both izzat (honour) and kamyaabi (success)." Another laments the status of the holy war vis-à-vis consumerism, saying: "It is a pity that the vision of some Muslims today has become confined to acquiring cars worth a few rupees (chand take ki gadi) and other goods of the temporary world."

While a police helicopter buzzes overhead, the Lashkar-e-Taiba activists sing jehadi nazms and the secretary-general of the Pakistan Hurriyat Conference, Ghulam Mohammed Shafi, criticises Nawaz Sharif and the Washington Declaration. "Mujhe mere doston se bachao, apne dushmano ko main khud dekh loonga," (Save me from my friends, I can look after my enemies myself), he laments.

Speaker after speaker criticises the withdrawal from Kargil. Ahmed Hamza, Amir of the Al-Badr Mujahideen, declares that "there can be no haggling over jehad." Zaki-ur-Rehman Lakhvi, chief commander of the Lashkar-e-Taiba, says, "Those who have sacrificed their brothers and sisters in Kashmir are wondering about what is happening today."

There is a deep sense of betrayal among the Lashkar leaders. Ali Hamza, leader of the Marqaz Dawa-ul-Irshad (the politico-religious organisation which has floated Lashkar-e-Taiba as its military wing) lashes out at Nawaz Sharif. "Mian has become the victim of a conspiracy," he declares.

Professor Hafiz Mohammed Sayeed, the head of Lashkar-e-Taiba, echoes his feelings, saying, "There isn't anyone as untrustworthy as America and Britain. Nor is there a bigger fool than someone who goes along with them." He asks Nawaz Sharif to repent as a Muslim for what he has done and seek the forgiveness of Allah while declaring that the jehad in Kashmir will continue "in Ladakh as well as in Doda and elsewhere." Remember, he says, "All roads for the mujahideen lead to Srinagar. Do not be disappointed. As long as there is even a single mujahideen alive, this holy war will continue."

There is a story doing the rounds in Islamabad though, that General Parvez Musharraf had been advised as early as in the first week of June by some of his friends that the Kargil operation was foolhardy. "You would have no option but to withdraw ultimately. So cut your losses even now. Tell Nawaz Sharif that the only way out is to tell the Indians that this has been a misadventure and that Pakistan should be given a way out of the situation. This would put the ball back in the Indian court and India would have a tough time refusing the request," he had apparently been told.

But appearing in sackcloth and ashes is not Nawaz Sharif's style. Even if he were to be forced to do so he was bound to avenge the insult by punishing those who had brought the situation upon him. General Musharraf apparently never put this proposal, which could have helped de-escalate the conflict in its early stages, to Nawaz Sharif. And perhaps fearing for his own future he also did not allow anyone else to present it to the prime minister. But like all juicy stories, this one too was difficult to verify.

The overwhelming feeling in Pakistan is that the Kargil operation was a miscalculation. "A poorly thought out and an ad hoc attempt to revive the Kashmir issue," was how former Pakistan foreign secretary Tanveer Ahmed Khan described the Kargil intrusions. But calling it a "miscalculation" is only a description of the failed strategy, I tell him, and it does not explain why it was embarked upon in the first place.

Sipping a cup of tea in the coffee shop of the Marriott Islamabad, Tanveer Ahmed Khan tries to explain to me why he thought Kargil happened. The full picture is not clear as yet, he admits. "But I see in it a vanishing hope in segments of Pakistani civil and military elite that a negotiated settlement with India over Kashmir is at all possible. There is a touch of desperation about the whole thing. The Lahore process, I would say, also invited a certain degree of distrust. I think that the fear of being 'betrayed', mistrust about the peace process, despondency about the possibility of any negotiated settlement of the Kashmir dispute plus the hope of internationalising Kashmir led to the Kargil manoeuvre," he explains.

The next day, I meet Lt. General (Retd.) Talat Masood, a former director-general of the Inter-Services Intelligence (ISI), in the same coffee shop. I thought the interview with him would go for a toss as the moment we sat down, in walked Ashraf Jehangir Qazi, the high commissioner of Pakistan in India and a friend of

General Masood. I thought General Masood would temper his views in front of Qazi but he was remarkably outspoken. Thankfully, Qazi left after quickly finishing his cup of coffee.

So why did Kargil happen, I prod General Masood. He explains patiently, "Pakistan considers itself an aggrieved party (in Kashmir). And therefore it tends to go for high-risk policies. The Kargil manoeuvre is part of that high-risk policy. There was a lack of synergy between the political and military elements in the sense that the likely political consequences were not fully debated. It is not true that the prime minister was not aware. This is not a case of denial of information. I attribute it to the lack of an institutional framework to discuss these things. That is why having a National Security Council is very important."

He was also of the view that Pakistan did not have the capacity to see the "Kargil manoeuvre" through. "Eventually the larger power prevails. There are wide disparities between India and Pakistan in terms of their conventional strength — both military and economic. However, the nuclear factor emboldened Pakistan to take a high risk. But the same factor also brought an unforeseen consequence — it raised the threshold very high immediately. It was a flawed manoeuvre. As soon as it happened, I knew that they would have to withdraw," he says.

General Masood feels that Pakistan should not have tried to project that the mujahideen alone were behind the Kargil operation — "They are not very popular with the world and created the impression of destabilising the region. The world would have taken a very different view if we had said that it was the mujahideen plus the Pakistani Army. After all, our cause is just. We have to be truthful about it."

Did he think that the Pakistani Army acquitted itself well in the Kargil episode? "The army has conducted itself very well. It is because of a lack of political coordination that it failed in its mission. But its role was excellent," he claims.

As luck would have it, General (Retd.) Jehangir Karamat also happened to be staying at the Marriott. An upright and thinking soldier, he had been sacked by Nawaz Sharif for suggesting that Pakistan should constitute a National Security Council — Sharif perhaps saw in this an attempt by the army to reassert its authority over the civilian executive. There had been rumours that the Kargil intrusion plan had been ready for a long time; that it had been put before Jehangir Karamat when he was the chief of army staff and that he had said in a lecture tour in America that he had thrown the plan out of the window for its sheer stupidity.

I asked someone who knew him whether General Karamat might agree to talk to me. He would not give an interview, I was told, but I could shake his hand. Well, I met him the next day in the lobby of the hotel. "It's an honour meeting a soldier like you, General. I have heard so much about you," I mumble politely. With a disarming smile, he says, "Nothing scandalous, I hope?" Later, a common friend told me that he had denied that the Kargil intrusion plan had ever been presented to him. Nor had he said in America that he had thrown the plan out of the window.

Talking to a cross-section of people in Islamabad and Rawalpindi, it was clear that the Kargil intrusions were a result of a belief, especially in the Pakistani Army, that unless the ground situation in Kashmir was changed, India would not come to the negotiating table. There was also an expectation that India would either react to the intrusions in the same way as it had done in the past — i.e. keep the whole thing low-key — or cross the Line of Control (LoC) and even open up a new front. The actual Indian reaction of deciding not to cross the LoC, chasing the intruders out using overwhelming force both in terms of men and materials, the induction of the air force, and not opening another battle front along the Indo-Pak border was not factored in by the Pakistanis.

Because the intrusions began last winter, the Pakistanis could not have accounted for the conflict taking place in an election year in India. "Your army was caught in a flap when it discovered the intrusions in May this year. Because it was caught unawares it over-reacted by inducting three divisions, keeping one of them in reserve and using the airforce. It suited the Bharatiya Janata Party to create war hysteria in the country because a mid-term election had been announced. The Indian Army played along. And your media also helped in fomenting war hysteria. There was no such hysteria in Pakistan," a senior defence analyst, who does not want to be identified, tells me.

The question, I ask him, still was why Pakistan opted for the Kargil strategy at a time when the world was applauding Nawaz Sharif as a man of peace. Just when the world was beginning to see India and Pakistan working towards a mutual nuclear restraint regime, why tell the world so dramatically that actually Pakistan is an irresponsible state, I ask him. "There has been an element of miscalculation in all this," he admits.

Ordering a beer in a hotel in Pakistan can take up to forty-five minutes — you have to establish that you are a foreigner and fill up forms in duplicate ordering the exact number of "units" of alcohol. Nazar Mohammed from the External Publicity Division of Pakistan knocks at my hotel room just when I have poured myself a glass of chilled Murry beer — after having completed the bureaucratic formalities of ordering two "units" of beer and giving the room-service waiter a photocopy of my passport. I wonder why he has come to see me so late — it is 8.30 at night and the person I am expecting is my old friend Major General (Retd.) Mahmud Ali Durrani. Durrani Sahib is to pick me up and take me to his son Usman's house for dinner.

"Did you get my message about the minister (Mushahid Hussain, the minister for information and broadcasting) meeting you at nine?" Nazar Mohammad asks me. I did, I tell him. He looks at my T-shirt and jeans before asking me hesitatingly, "Then you are ready to see the minister? Will you come like this?" "Of course not. I will have a shower and put on a suit to see the minister," I tell him. "But it is already past 8.30, sir. There is no time for all that." We look at each other till it dawns on me that while I thought I was to see Mushahid Hussain at nine the next morning, the appointment is tonight. "But you said nau baje (nine o'clock). You didn't say nau baje raat ko (nine pm)," I complain.

I tell him I had committed to go for dinner with General Durrani and that this appointment was fixed even before I had left India. I can't mess around with him, I tell him. Now Nazar Mohammed is clearly upset. I plead with him to call Mushahid Hussain's residence. There is no problem, Mushahid Hussain says, "Come for lunch tomorrow."

As I get into General Durrani's car, he turns to his wife Fatima and says, "You were asking me how I can call an Indian a friend. Well, here he is. Ask him whatever you wanted to ask him." His shocked wife goes red in the face and protests by saying, "But when did I say that? I never said such a thing."

"Come on, come on, there is no need to be shy about these things. A lot of people here think like you do. I want you to know that Indians don't have tails. That is why I wanted you to meet Bharat. You can ask him all the questions you keep asking me about India," he says, as I hand him a small woven Kashmiri

In the 'Enemy Country'

carpet that I had brought from India for him. "General Sahib, you can never have Kashmir. But you can keep a piece of it under your feet," I tell him. He laughs out loud saying, "Tumne badmashi nahin chhodi" (You have not stopped being mischievous). His wife, he tells me, is originally from Srinagar. Her family still has a house overlooking the Dal Lake, she tells me. "You should come to Srinagar and visit your ancestral home," I say. "Insha Allah," she replies politely.

Over dinner, we don't discuss Kargil so much as Indian and Pakistani stereotypes of each other. We discuss *Sarfarosh,* a slick Mumbai Hindi film that reinforces the image of Pakistanis as untrustworthy and cunning. I am told that a lot of Pakistanis think the same of India and Indians.

The topic of conversation moves to a common acquaintance, Najam Sethi, editor of *Friday Times.* He had been kidnapped, tortured and confined by the Pakistani security agencies for criticising the Pakistani establishment in a lecture in India. "But had he not delivered the same lecture at the GHQ in Rawalpindi and the entire army brass had given him a standing ovation?" I ask. "May be. But saying the same thing in the enemy country is an entirely different matter," says Usman, the general's son and my host of the evening. "Usman, don't use such phrases in front of Bharat at least. He is our guest," General Durrani gently reprimands him. "No, no. It's OK. I have heard the phrase in India too," I protest.

Indeed, I was to hear it again and again in the wake of the Kargil episode. "Sir, do you think the Reserve Bank of India will give us permission readily to send money to our stringer in the enemy country," one of our senior accounts managers was to ask me a week later. He was inquiring about how to pay an occasional contributor I had engaged on behalf of my newspaper in Islamabad.

Mushahid Hussain's bungalow is a red brick structure, like the rest of the bungalows in Islamabad's Ministers' Enclave — an enclosed high security area. "Have the grilled trout. I got it from Gilgit," Mushahid Hussain says, serving me a fillet. "Did you catch it yourself?" I ask him. "No, no, no. Somebody gave it to me," he replies. Mushahid is a charming person except when he is spouting anti-India statements on television.

There are only two of us at lunch. Mushahid Hussain, the excellent host that he is, keeps piling food on my plate describing every dish as "very light". Was he watching his weight like I was, I wonder. He perhaps would have to, I say to myself, if he has to keep Nawaz Sharif company whose penchant for eating parathas, nihari (a broth of trotters and goat's tongue) and gajrela (a variant of carrot-halwa) is legendary.

"Try these cherries. These are also from the northern areas," Mushahid Hussain offers me a bowl full of cherries so ripe that they look black. Looks like I am in for a Kashmir-special lunch. "And have some mango too," he says. I hope to myself that he does not go into the usual spiel about how Pakistani mangoes are better than Indian ones and the virtues of Anwar Ratol mangoes over Indian ones. Thankfully he does not do that and instead makes some polite queries about common journalist friends in India.

After lunch, we settle down to discuss Kargil. "Kargil is a consequence of India's flawed Kashmir policy. As long as the Kashmir issue is not resolved, these situations will arise," he declares.

Do you expect anyone to believe that the Kargil operation was initiated and conducted by the so-called mujahideen, I ask him. "The mujahideen have been known for their brilliant initiatives. Pakistan does not remote-control them and it has no direct authority over them except that of moral, friendly persuasion. What the mujahideen have done in Indian-held Kashmir is akin to what the

In the 'Enemy Country'

Hezbullah did in Israel to influence Israeli policy towards Lebanon. These things happen in guerilla warfare. The mujahideen have demonstrated that the Kashmir issue cannot be brushed away. You can no longer stage Hamlet without the Prince of Denmark. The insurgency is not over. After Kargil, it could be Baramulla and the Valley next. The message from Kargil is that the mujahideen can take any action anywhere," he declares.

I ask him about the domestic fallout from the withdrawal from Kargil. "Nobody here believed that Kargil would lead to the liberation of Kashmir. It internationalised Kashmir, the Indian Army got a hammering and Kashmir has become the number one issue in Indian politics today. The basic message that has emanated from this conflict is that there is now an inextricable linkage between Kashmir and durable peace in South Asia. All this (has been) achieved in a matter of six weeks!" Mushahid Hussain boasts.

So, he says, "There has been an element of satisfaction over the mujahideen struggle as well as what Nawaz Sharif did to internationalise it. He talked for three hours on Kashmir with President Bill Clinton."

But Nawaz Sharif does not seem to have much public support for what he has done, I point out. "The electorate of Pakistan is clear on one bottomline — that whatever happens, war should be prevented because irrespective of who wins or loses, the economies suffer and so does the Kashmir issue. There is no war constituency in Pakistan today. This is a very big achievement. Only Nawaz Sharif could have done this. The proof of the pudding is in the fact that there have been no demonstrations in the streets (against Nawaz Sharif). And it wasn't as if there was any lack of attempt by others to exploit the situation," he answers.

Would it be possible to see the prime minister, I ask him. Mushahid's assessment is that Nawaz Sharif is unlikely to give an interview at this juncture. "But would you like to join him for cricket? I could fix that." He picks up the phone and asks someone, "What is Mian Sahib's programme? Koi khel-kood ka programme hai?" (Any plan for sports?). He promises to get back to me on this.

The pullout from Kargil was not very popular with the people of Pakistan. In popular perception, it was being seen as peace without honour and the extremists were dubbing it as a sellout to the Americans. Anti-American sentiment in Pakistan by far outstripped anti-Indian sentiment.

There was a feeling that Nawaz Sharif's decision had damaged Pakistani national pride and disappointed the mujahideen; that a tactical victory had been converted into a strategic defeat; that the image of the Pakistani Army had been tarnished and that it was being described now as a "rogue army"; that the mujahideen heeding the advice of Pakistan to withdraw had meant "confessing too much" to the world about Pakistani involvement with them; that the retreat from Kargil carried the danger of going too far — as it might lead to the crystallisation of international opinion on the LoC as the international border between India and Pakistan; and lastly, that having sacrificed lives to defend its side of the LoC, the Indian position on the Kashmir issue would now harden and that it might never cede territory defended by blood.

There could be no doubt that Pakistani society was in turmoil over what happened in Kargil. However, nobody wanted to blame the Pakistani Army for this misadventure. Even liberal elements in Pakistani society who thought that the Kargil operation was foolish, displayed an ostrich-like attitude, saying that the army should not be brought into any controversy.

The army chief had publicly declared that Nawaz Sharif was fully on board when the operation was planned and that the

In the 'Enemy Country'

decision to withdraw from Kargil was a political one. And the prime minister claimed that it was at President Bill Clinton's request that he had appealed to the mujahideen to withdraw from Kargil. Ergo, everyone blamed America for something for which heads should have rolled domestically.

I ask Khalid Mahmud, a former Pakistani journalist and now a fellow with the Institute of Regional Analysis in Islamabad, if he thought Nawaz Sharif was kept in the dark by the army about the Kargil operation and how it was that the army accepted the withdrawal quietly.

Khalid Mahmud lights up a cigarette, takes a deep puff and says, "Look, it is not possible for the army to plan such an operation without the information and consent of the prime minister. But it is quite possible that this was an army initiative and Nawaz Sharif did not comprehend its full implications. The army may have agreed to Nawaz Sharif's call for withdrawal but this must have caused heartburn and disappointment — particularly among the junior officers. While there is no chance of an imminent conflict between the army and the prime minister, one cannot rule out discontent."

Many in Pakistan believe that in the wake of the Kargil episode, both Prime Minister Nawaz Sharif and the army chief, General Pervez Musharraf, have been considerably weakened. The Americans, the Pakistanis feel, do not want a military coup. Therefore, they argue, the relationship that has developed between the army and the civilian executive over the last two years, with the former subjecting itself to the control of the latter, is unlikely to change. Nawaz Sharif has an overwhelming majority in the National Assembly and under normal circumstances he can be expected to continue in office till the next general election unless he is replaced before that by someone from within his own party, the Pakistan Muslim League. Even those sympathetic to him admit, however, that in the long run the Kargil episode will erode his support base and credibility.

Lt. General (Retd.) Hammed Gul is no supporter of Prime Minister Nawaz Sharif. He was described to me by one of his colleagues as "a man with a cause in search of a party". The former ISI chief, credited with his deep involvement in Afghanistan, is one of the few Pakistanis who has refused to see me in person. "You can put your questions to me over the phone," he says.

"Nawaz Sharif has lost the moral mandate to govern," General Gul declares over the telephone. "His action has divided the nation. The response to the withdrawal from Kargil, you will see, will build up over time. The political initiative will pass into the hands of the religious parties. Nawaz Sharif will be running like a hare. It is only international pressure that is shoring him up," he claims.

I had rung up an old acquaintance, a sympathiser of Pakistan Peoples' Party, and asked whether we could meet. I drive to Rawalpindi for the meeting. Over cups of sabz chai (green tea), we discuss Nawaz Sharif. "The Kargil debate has to play itself out. It is too early to say how this will impact on civil-military relations or on the credibility of Nawaz Sharif. But he is a much diminished man today because of the humiliating manner in which this crisis has ended," she says.

But does she think that the Kargil episode will push Pakistan towards the religious Right — after all they are the only groups who are bringing people onto the streets while the established political parties are unable to mobilise even a dozen people against the government, I ask. "Under Nawaz Sharif's repressive mode of governance, the political middle ground has shrunk in this country. He is driving the country towards a more extremist direction — this is what the attempt to enforce the Sharia Bill was all about. He is creating a fertile ground for regional as well as religious extremists and possibly a deadly mixture of the two. This undermines the very basis of Pakistan's existence," she replies.

"This environment has been created by the Nawaz Sharif government in the last one year. They thought they were being clever in adopting the agenda of these people (the religious extremists). But they should know that this is the slippery slope of compromise," she says. Added to this, the declining economy of Pakistan with its large pools of the unemployed and the underemployed provides a conducive context for the growth of extremists of all kinds, she laments.

She thinks that one of the fundamental problems of the Pakistani state was its inability to recognise the domestic fallout from certain types of international behaviour in the region. Thus, she points out, the first phase of Pakistan's Afghan policy, leading to the ouster of the Russians, led to the drugs and gun-culture in Pakistan. And the second phase of the policy, followed in the post-Taliban Afghanistan, has fuelled extremist religious forces and sectarian Shia-Sunni violence in Pakistan, she claims. "You can reverse this now, but not ten years down the line. We should realise that the politics of expediency leads to the law of unforeseen consequences," she says.

Indeed, there are some Pakistani intellectuals who fear that Pakistan is getting "communalised" — moving towards a more politically militant form of Islam — and that it is suffering from a crisis of identity. As one of them tells me, "The Pakistani identity is a reactive identity — the identity of the part that broke away from the whole. The very religious forces (the Deobandis) which had opposed the formation of Pakistan now want to push an Islamic fundamentalist theocratic identity on Pakistan. They leave it undefined but pack it with a great deal of passion. There is an attempt to superimpose an all-encompassing Islamic identity on different ethnicities."

What is worse is that the so-called mujahideen are being actively supported by sections of the Pakistani state. As long as they are directed outwards — towards Afghanistan, Kashmir, Chechnya or Xinxiang — their ideology can be seen as export-oriented Islamic terrorism. But what happens when they turn inwards? Says Azziz Siddiqui, former editor of *The Frontier Post* and now joint director of the Human Rights Commission of Pakistan, "After coming back from Kargil, where will these people go? They will only turn inwards. They may not amount to much with respect to India but they will become a great problem for Pakistan. They find allies in the government and possibly even in the army."

Nawaz Sharif, feels Siddiqui, deliberately chooses to go along with the religious fundamentalists despite his majority in the National Assembly — "He does this partly because of conviction and partly because he thinks he needs them politically."

He refers to an "honour killing" of a woman seeking a divorce from her abusive husband, carried out in broad daylight in the office of noted civil rights lawyer Hina Jillani in Lahore on 6 April this year. The murder was allegedly carried out at her father's behest.

"The government has not been able to produce a challan in court. Even a resolution condemning the act could not be passed in the Senate because the representatives from the North-West Frontier Province, and quite disappointingly, even those belonging to the Awami National Party opposed it and made shameful speeches. It is clear that these fundamentalists have the backing of the institutions of the state. Unfortunately, we cannot underestimate the influence of these people. After all at Muridke, the Lashkar-e-Taiba is running a state within a state in Punjab. There are lunatic fringes everywhere but they must remain on the fringes. If they have the support of the state then it is dangerous. That is what makes it very difficult for me to be optimistic," he says.

Are things that bad? Is there no ray of hope, I ask him. "The only slight ray of hope is the human instinct for survival. If the Lahore process is advanced, even if for the sheer narrow political purposes of the ruling elite, then at least a disaster can be averted," he claims.

Abdullah Muntazer is one of the public faces of Lashkar-e-Taiba. He is the information secretary of the organisation. He is remarkably young — perhaps in his late twenties. He has a flowing beard and wears a grey Pathan suit with the salwar ending well above his ankles, a new symbol of the "pious" — separating the jehadis from the ordinary Muslims of Pakistan.

"We don't want friendship with India because it is not practical," he announces. He drops another bomb by saying, "The BJP suits us. Within a year they have made us into a nuclear power and a missile power. The Lashkar-e-Taiba is getting a good response because of the BJP's statements. It is much better than before. We pray to God that they come to power again because then we will emerge even stronger."

Abdullah Muntazer has come to my hotel room to be interviewed along with his deputy who is even younger than him — a twenty-year-old commerce graduate from Dera-Ismail Khan. Muntazer is educated and proceeds to inform me that he reads Indian newspapers on the internet every day. He says that he received his guerrilla training in Pakistan-occupied Kashmir (PoK).

Muntazer declares that the aim of his organisation is to

implement Islam in the whole world — "by preaching where possible and through jehad where necessary. In Pakistan we will preach. But in India we will conduct a jehad," he tells me.

But why a jehad in India? "Because you are aggressive and cruel. If you cannot tolerate the Muslims of Kashmir, how will you ever tolerate the Muslims in the rest of India?" he asks. When pressed, he grudgingly admits that "some Muslims may be happy in India but we do meet people who claim that they are discriminated against."

He then proceeds to clarify that Lashkar-e-Taiba's programme was very different from that of other militant Islamic organisations in Kashmir. "The others want to liberate Kashmir and participate in governing it. We want to make Kashmir our base camp and then conduct a jehad in the rest of India," he says without batting an eyelid.

Why did you murder Border Security Force personnel in Bandipura (in July this year), I ask him. "The BSF is killing Muslims. What is the life of one deputy inspector-general of police in comparison? We will take revenge for each of the seventy thousand Muslims killed in Kashmir," he declares.

I put it to him that since his organisation's concept of jehad was all-encompassing and since the majority in Pakistan seemed happy not supporting the Lashkar-e-Taiba, would his organisation therefore advocate jehad even in Pakistan? "Nobody wants to set his own house on fire through an armed jehad. We are aware that Pakistan is not following the teachings of Allah. But we do not consider jehad proper against fellow Muslims," he replies.

I ask him why his organisation does not want to find out whether or not the people of Pakistan want its brand of Islam by participating in the democratic electoral process. "But democracy is a parallel system to Islam and the two are opposed to each other," he exclaims. "We don't believe in democracy. The government cannot be of the people. Only Allah Tala has the right to governance. Laws have been laid down in the Hadees and the Holy Koran and no parliament can be given the right to make law. The majority is the authority in democracy, but what if the majority consists of the badmash and the goondas? There are many faults in this system."

Asked about the practical ways in which democracy could be changed by the Lashkar-e-Taiba in Pakistan or elsewhere, Muntazer replies enigmatically, "When you churn buttermilk, the butter comes up by itself. Islamic preaching and jehad will churn society and Insha Allah (God Willing) the butter of khilafat (Rule of the Caliph, associated with rule based on Islam) will come up." How soon did he expect this to happen? "There is no time frame for these things. Allah says leave the result to me," he replies.

I ask the twenty-year-old colleague of Abdullah Muntazer who sits quietly through the interview about what his family thought of what he was doing in the Lashkar. "They are very happy," he says. Was he ever going to get a proper job, I ask him. "My needs such as food, clothes and jooties (shoes) are taken care of by the organisation. I have no other needs," he replies. How about getting married some day, I ask him. "I would prefer to marry the sister of someone in the organisation. This is what others in the organisation do. But Hafeez Mohammad Sayeed (the head of the Lashkar) will take care of this. He treats us like his own children," he replies.

This is the age when he ought to be having fun and enjoying himself instead of getting mixed up with people who tell you that having fun is bad, I pull his leg. He tells me with a sombre face that he has devoted his life to Islam (Deen ka kaam kar rahe hain).

Why are you so hard on yourself and the people around you, I ask Abdullah Muntazer. Why do you tell people that they should not listen to music or clap to express happiness or smoke a cigarette? He has an "answer" for everything. Music is the voice of Satan (Gana-bajana Shaitan ki awaz hai), he tells me. But what about the greatness of Sufi music? "Sufis are close to the Hindus," he explains. And what could be wrong with clapping, I ask him. "Taali bajana (clapping) is for women — Auraton ka kaam hai. In Islam men are forbidden from clapping," Muntazer claims.

How about smoking unless you are trying to prevent cancer, I ask. Without getting upset, he replies, "Islam mein nasha haram hai" (Islam forbids any form of intoxication). And is it proper to carry arms? "Asla to Musalman ka zevar hai (Arms are like wearing jewels for a Muslim). They are the guarantors of peace," he speaks with the raw confidence normally found in strategic experts defending nuclear deterrence.

With the interview over, Muntazer tells me not to take the same elevator to the hotel lobby. We will take a different route, he says while we get into two facing elevators. When I reach the lobby, I find that he has disappeared — perhaps through the service entrance.

"So what is this letter you are carrying from our prime minister to Nawaz Sharif?" Indian High Commissioner G. Parthasarathy asks me. "What letter? What are you talking about?" I ask him totally bewildered. "As a journalist you must at least read the Urdu press here carefully. The daily *Ausaf* has a front page boxed report saying that after R.K. Mishra's diplomatic forays now you are carrying a letter from Vajpayee to Nawaz Sharif," he tells me. I had gone to meet the high commissioner over a cup of tea.

"If the government of India needs journalists to carry messages to Pakistan, why do they have a full-fledged High Commission in Islamabad? You can shut shop and leave India-Pakistan relations to journalists," I joke with him.

But I am angry enough to call the editor of *Ausaf*, Hamid Mir, and ask him what this is all about. "This is what our reporter felt when he met you asking for an interview," he replies. But all that I had told the *Ausaf* reporter was that I was a reporter like him and that I interviewed people for my newspaper instead of giving interviews myself. "He somehow thought that there was more to your refusal than this," Hamid Mir says.

"Listen, do you want me to lose my job? Do you think it is a matter of pride for an independent journalist to be described as the messenger-boy of the government of the day? How would you like it if you came to India on assignment and I wrote a similar report about you in my paper?" I shout at him. He promises amends and invites me for a cup of tea.

Ausaf is a jehadi newspaper — reflecting the views of the religious fundamentalist organisations and the armed forces, or so I have been told. Hamid Mir is remarkably young — perhaps in his late thirties. If he had not been sitting in the editor's office, he could pass off as a local goonda whose path you may not want to cross. From his body language it is clear that he understands both power and politics. He has a remarkably clear mind. He makes no bones about his sympathies for the religio-political organisations and the army but at the same time wants them to keep the executive in check and not displace it altogether.

"My Kashmir perspective may be close to that of the Lashkar-e-Taiba, but I don't want them occupying the Prime Minister's office," he declares. He is opposed to the Washington Declaration which had led Nawaz Sharif to withdraw from Kargil. "The Jamat-e-Islami consisting of the Shias, Sunnis, Deobandis and even Barelvis is opposed to it. The Pak Awami Tehreek consisting largely of the

Barelvis is also opposed to it. The Jamiat Ulema Islam has adopted an ambivalent position because it is an ally of the government and a part of the provincial government in Balochistan. Otherwise there is a consensus in the nation on opposing the Washington Declaration. The Nawaz Sharif government is cornered and sidelined. There is a political vacuum waiting to be filled," he tells me.

Who does he think will fill this vacuum, I ask him. "The people first tested Benazir. She could not deliver for a variety of reasons. Then they brought in Nawaz Sharif. He has also failed. In this situation, the right wing parties and religious groups have got strengthened. For the first time, a militant organisation involved in Kashmir (Lashkar-e-Taiba) is organising meetings challenging the government in the Federal Capital and in Lahore at Mochi Gate, where Pakistani political parties used to hold their rallies. And the government can do nothing. The situation has become quite complicated because Nawaz Sharif just cannot control the militants. After the Washington Declaration, he had to call a meeting of the Jehad Council, representing the organisations fighting in Kashmir along with the director general of ISI and the chief of army staff. And in that meeting the commanders of the Hizbul Mujahideen and Harkat-ul-Mujahideen, told him point blank that they were not going to withdraw from Kargil," he replies.

I ask him how he thinks the political scenario is going to unfold. He thinks that the right-wing parties may come into power "but there is no threat of Talibanisation." He then proceeds to give me reasons why Pakistan will not get Talibanised. "What you see in Afghanistan is a manifestation of their culture not their religion. For example, long beards and women in burkhas are fairly common in the sections of society the Taliban come from. A similar culture may exist in our North-West Frontier Province, in the tribal society of Balochistan but not in Punjab and certainly not in

In the 'Enemy Country'

Sindh. Central and southern Punjab is a Sufi area. In Sindh people will beat you up with shoes if you so much as even take the name of the Taliban before them," he argues.

Have there been no attempts to push the Taliban ideology in Pakistan, I ask him. "In Kohat, Bannoo and Lakki Marwat, south of the NWFP, some students did try a bit of the Taliban medicine — breaking television sets and uprooting antennae. The people beat them up. Maulana Fazlur Rehman, chief of the Jamiat Ulema Islam, the patron of the Taliban in Pakistan, told these students to shut up and recognise the differences between the Afghan and Pakistani societies."

The next day, I am relieved to find that Hamid Mir has published a correction on the front page of *Ausaf* saying that what they had written the previous day was wrong and that I was in Pakistan in pursuit of my professional duties. He ascribed the previous day's report to a galatfahami (misunderstanding).

Majid Nizami, in his light green summer suit, sits flanked by portraits of Mohammad Ali Jinnah, the founder of Pakistan, and Hamid Nizami, the founder of *Nawa-i-Waqt*. There is a model of Minar-e-Pakistan on the book-case behind him. Jinnah, Hamid Nizami, *Nawa-i-Waqt and* Minar-e-Pakistan are inextricably linked.

When the Pakistan Resolution was moved on 23 March 1940 by the Muslim League at the spot where the Minar-e-Pakistan is now situated, Hamid Nizami was one of those who was present. To commemorate the occasion, he had launched *Nawa-i-Waqt*.

"It was not right to invite Atal Behari Vajpayee to Lahore. We were opposed to Vajpayee coming to Lahore and that too in a special dosti ki (friendship) bus. He should have been invited to the political capital that is Islamabad where friends and foes both are welcomed. Why should he have come to Lahore where the Pakistan resolution was moved? Lahore to Pakistan ka dil hai" (Lahore is the heart of Pakistan), says Majid Nizami, the chief editor and owner of *Nawa-i-Waqt*.

"Dosti dil se hi to hoti hai" (But friendship must appeal to the heart), I tell him. "Friendships don't happen in a day," Nizami retorts. "Kashmir comes in the way of Indo-Pak friendship. If Vajpayee does not want to solve the Kashmir dispute then how can there be any friendship between the two countries? If Nawaz Sharif extends the hand of friendship to India without resolving the Kashmir issue, it would only go to show that he is totally shameless."

"We are opposed to the bus-diplomacy tooth and nail. And we are now opposing this Ailan-e-Washington (the Washington Declaration). Nawaz Sharif is blackmailing the electorate by talking about averting a war with India. I didn't see any signs of war. He got an interview with Clinton through Saudi Arabia, I think. But let me tell you the Americans wanted to punish him — not for Kargil but for the 28 May nuclear explosion... (The Americans believe that) you have got to get personal punishment — Bhutto was hanged and Zia got burnt alive in an aircrash. I don't know what kind of punishment Nawaz Sharif will get," he says, elaborating on his thesis of why the US seems to have swung its weight in favour of India during the Kargil crisis.

I am getting late for my flight back to India. As I drive to the airport, I think of Majid Nizami. It is hardcore anti-India elements like him who need to be convinced by the Pakistani establishment that there is a need to work towards better relations with India. I remember a story that someone had told me. Nawaz Sharif apparently had not wanted to conduct any nuclear tests to match India's tests last May. "Why should I test when Clinton was on the phone every day promising to open his treasury for

Pakistan?" he is believed to have told his confidantes. Majid Nizami, running one of the most powerful newspapers in the country, apparently rang him up and told him that if he did not test, he himself would be blown away politically. Although confirmed by a friend of his, I wish I had remembered to cross-check this with Nizami himself.

The meeting with Nizami has taken far too long. I haven't even had time to have lunch. As I check out of the Pearl Continental, my driver tells me that he knows a very nice place for lunch on the way to the airport. He takes me to Lahore's brand new McDonald's. Then he drives me at breakneck speed to the airport. He has been with me throughout my stay in Lahore. He hugs me goodbye and says, "Next time please bring bhabiji (meaning my wife) along and ask for me by name at the hotel." As I slip him his tip, he accepts it reluctantly saying, "There is no need for this. Tusi to sade pra ho" (You are our brother). After a fratricidal war in Kargil, somehow it is nice to hear this.

AN EMOTIONAL ASSIGNMENT

■ SAURABH DAS

> For the photojournalist with Associated Press, Kargil was not just a professional assignment but an emotional one. He felt deeply moved by the plight of the soldiers and the refugees and focussed on the tragedy of the war.

The Kargil assignment was unique for me: with India fighting a war I wasn't just a professional photographer there... there was emotion I felt as an Indian. It did affect my work — I would feel numbed, drained of all emotion at the end of the day, especially in the first few weeks of the war, which were bad for the Indian Army. It was disheartening as an Indian to listen to the soldiers' tales of woe — they were absolutely unprepared and had to climb heights of fifteen thousand to eighteen thousand feet without proper clothing in freezing temperatures. It was also frustrating for me as a professional as we were not allowed to actually see the war. I neither had the will nor the scope, therefore, to be "artistic" — what's artistic about a Bofors gun being fired to kill people?

What I mostly focussed on was the destruction that the war was causing — the tragedy of it. The looks on the faces of the refugees fleeing with their belongings still haunt me. And the soldiers were a revelation — they faced death and worked absurd hours, driven only by the desire to liberate the peaks. It takes a lot of courage to return from an assault on one peak only to go on another such assault all over again. Of course the jawans and the officers were also openly critical of the military leadership for creating this mess in the first place, and of the fact that they had to fight the war with their hands tied behind their backs, as they could not cross the Line of Control. I found them to be very, very brave and thorough gentlemen. But faced with the enemy, the same soldiers were capable of barbaric acts too... Covering the war underlined for me yet again the futility of violence.

A Pakistani shell lands on a TV relay centre being used by the Indian army for Signal Corps in Drass.

A Bofors gun firing at enemy targets in the Drass sector.

A lieutenant tries to figure out the impact of his Bofors gun used in the direct firing mode in Mushkoh valley.

Soldiers and journalists running away from Pakistani shelling at Pandrass (above) *and taking shelter in a bunker* (facing page).

A soldier laughs at his newly-recruited colleague who has ducked to avoid being hit, even though the shells have landed pretty far off, in Bimbet, near Drass.

Soldiers back from the peaks at Mushkoh valley rest under a truck.

A soldier's body is brought back to New Delhi with full military honours.

Prime Minister Atal Behari Vajpayee in a pensive mood as he, accompanied by Army Chief V.P. Malik, meets soldiers in Kargil.

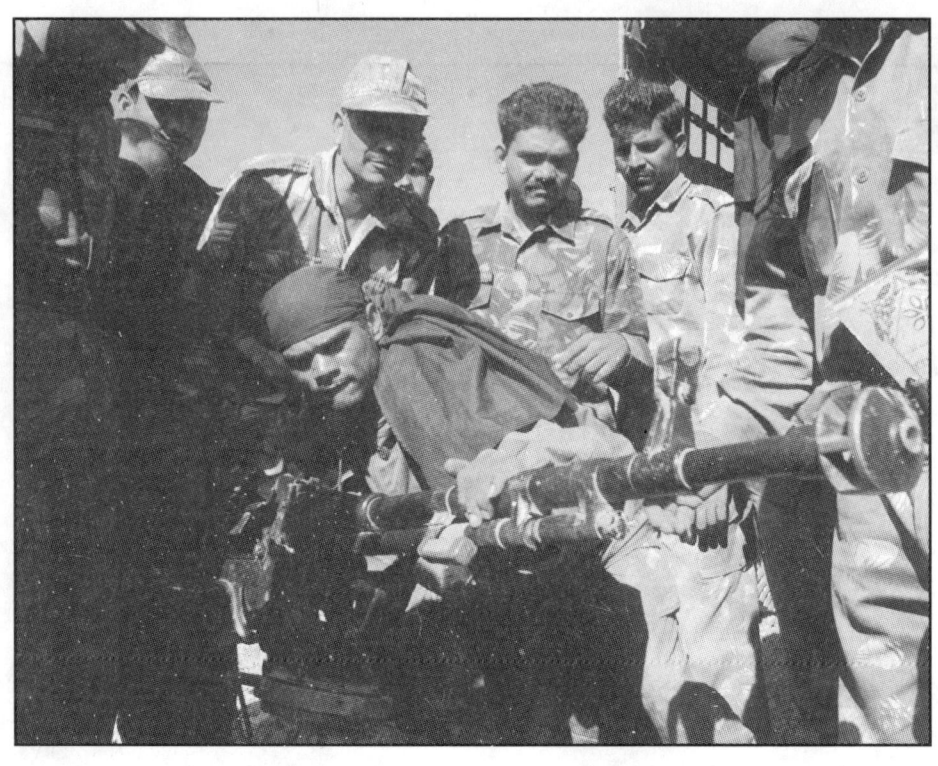

A soldier poses with a captured Pakistani gun (above) *in Mushkoh valley. And seized Pakistani arms and ammunition* (facing page) *being brought down for display from recaptured peaks.*

A Drass family (above) *flees Kargil. And refugees from Kargil* (facing page) *waiting for supplies under the shadow of the gun at Mingee.*

Refugees waiting to be evacuated in the Drass sector.

A Dismal Failure

■ Rahul Bedi

> The Kargil war was a miserable intelligence and military failure, argues the India correspondent of *Jane's Defence Weekly*. The jawans and officers who fought in Kargil want heads to roll, but that is unlikely to happen.

A Dismal Failure

India's avoidable border war with Pakistan in Kargil, like the 1962 debacle against the Chinese, ranks as a dismal intelligence and military failure. The intrusion by hundreds of Pakistani soldiers and Islamic mercenaries led to eleven weeks of bitter fighting that ended around mid-July, in which nearly twelve hundred men, including 487 Indian soldiers, died. Another eleven hundred Indian soldiers were maimed, half of them permanently.

The Indian Army further compounded the grievous error by its inability to assess either the seriousness or the extent of the intrusion along 120 km to 140 km of the LoC almost three weeks after it was discovered in early May in the Kargil sector.

Senior commanders initially portrayed the intrusion as an infiltration by a "handful of foreign mercenaries" being pumped in by Pakistan to bolster Kashmir's decade-long civil war for an independent Islamic homeland in which over twenty-five thousand people have died, and issued orders for them to be dealt with accordingly. This, in turn, led to panicky officers despatching ill-equipped and unacclimatised troops on "suicide missions" up sheer mountain slopes over sixteen thousand feet high to dislodge the strategically entrenched enemy.

"Senior commanders were unwilling to give credence to the growing certainty that a large portion of Indian territory had actually been captured by Pakistan," an officer said. For instance, the military's initial assessment for Tiger Hill, the 16,400 feet high feature that dominates the region and which ultimately took nearly two months of arduous campaigning to recapture, was that it was unoccupied or, at worst, held by a few Afghan mercenaries. A war game staged earlier in the year by senior commanders had dismissed the possibility of Tiger Hill being occupied as "ridiculous," an option not even worth considering.

Uninformed and badly-equipped troops of 1 Naga and 8 Sikh

regiments were launched up mountain slopes with orders to bring down the intruders "by the scruff of their necks" from atop Tiger Hill. To their amazement the two units came under withering fire from universal machine guns, 122 mm mortars, rocket-propelled grenades and anti-aircraft guns and took heavy losses.

Outnumbered, many patrols were surrounded and shot dead. After nearly three weeks of repeated assaults that were mercilessly beaten back, 1 Naga's losses totalled eighty dead and wounded. Other units suffered a similarly high casualty rate, till realisation dawned on the senior commanders as to how serious the intrusion actually was. This ultimately led to around eighteen artillery regiments or over hundred guns, including the Bofors FH77 155 mm Howitzers, being rushed to the area, panic buying of high-altitude gear and an overall change in strategy that involved rushing around fifty-eight battalions involved in fighting armed separatists in the Kashmir Valley to the front and calling in the air force.

When the enemy was finally evicted from around fifteen hundred sq km of Indian territory following savage battles, some lasting several weeks, 487 Indian soldiers, including twenty-five officers, had died. Also killed were seven hundred Pakistanis, mainly soldiers from the Northern Light Infantry (NLI) and units like the Gilgit and Huza Scouts as well as Islamic mercenaries.

In battle after decisive battle Indian infantry battalions clambered up near perpendicular cliffs the entire night in freezing temperatures before lunging straight into battle at first light against the intruders who, undisturbed, had fortified themselves across high ridges and behind cleverly crafted cement and stone bunkers, some of them two to three storeys high. Surviving on cigarettes, biscuits and pieces of ice, infantry units crawled up icy walls before attacking the advantageously placed NLI on ridges between fifteen thousand and seventeen thousand feet high. The Indian

A Dismal Failure

Army — as also the Indian Air Force (IAF) after it joined the fray on 26 May — were further disadvantaged in not being able to cross the LoC to cut off the intruders' supply lines inside Pakistan-administered Kashmir. To have done so would have escalated the conflict between the two nuclear-capable countries.

Daylight activity was suicidal as any movement against the white, snowy background was instantly visible and invited devastating fire from the intruders above. There were even instances of Indian attacks being beaten back by the enemy rolling boulders down precipitous hillsides. One officer said each fighting infantryman needed a backup of around five men to secure climbing ropes and keep ammunition and supply lines open.

Indian officials acknowledge that the enemy had done its job well. "It was a methodical operation planned meticulously by professionals," said a senior Indian military officer. It has now been learnt that Pakistan also transported three 105 mm field guns onto Point 4833, some five km inside Indian territory between Drass and Mushkoh, which played havoc for nearly two months, firing on Indian Army locations and the militarily crucial Highway 1A between Srinagar and Leh — the staging point for the Siachen glacier, occupied by India since 1984 — and the frontier with China.

Artillery pieces weighing around twelve hundred kg each were dismantled and the pieces flown in by helicopters by Pakistan. "The enemy used innovative techniques in flying its helicopters along the nape of the valleys along mountain peaks, careful not to be visible against the horizon," one officer said. The Pakistanis also carved the mountain sides, probably by dynamiting portions of it, to accommodate the field guns. Ultimately, a raiding party from the Naga regiment scaled the Mushkoh peak and silenced the field pieces.

The 776 km long LoC stretching from the international border in the Jammu region in the plains to the fourteen thousand feet high Zojila Pass at the end of the Kashmir Valley, is well guarded. But the 180-200 km long stretch of the LoC, from Zojila Pass to Khor, which lies beyond Leh remains relatively undefended. The remaining seventy-five km of the disputed Siachen glacial area completes Kashmir's frontier with Pakistan and China.

Snaking its way through a snowy, mountainous wasteland up to nearly eighteen thousand feet, criss-crossed by ridges and deep valleys, this area is the world's second coldest place after Siberia and is under fifteen to twenty feet of snow between October and June. Temperatures here average around twenty degrees celsius below zero, falling to minus sixty degrees celsius in winter with a wind-chill factor of formidable intensity. Consequently, there had traditionally been no infiltration of militants from this barren stretch. Over the years the army made do with observation posts spaced along the LoC that were manned by infrequent patrols for around four months after the snows melted in June. "That was exactly what attracted Pakistan," said an army officer.

He said Pakistan had long wanted to dominate National Highway 1 A that meanders alongside the LoC — at a distance of five to twelve km away from it — in order to choke all traffic between Srinagar and Leh by saturating it with artillery fire and thus effectively isolating Ladakh. The LoC, delineated on nineteen maps after the 1971 war, provides Pakistan only a small "window" onto the crucial highway. But seizing control of the area where the conflict raged gave Pakistani artillery clear access to the highway, throttling all movement along it. If Pakistan had succeeded in interdicting the highway it could easily have handicapped all future Indian Army deployments in the Ladakh region as supply and troop convoys would have been forced to

A Dismal Failure

make suicidal dashes along it or spend days, even weeks, winding their circuitous way to Leh via Manali in the neighbouring Himachal Pradesh state.

"India may have pushed back the Pakistani invasion," an army officer said, "but it has lost the battle as it frantically prepares for the formidable and hugely expensive task of permanently manning the LoC to prevent future intrusions." Official sources estimate it would cost around ten crore a day to maintain around eight thousand to ten thousand soldiers of 8 Mountain Division from Mushkoh valley (the western point of the LoC) to Chorbatla (the eastern point). India already spends about three crore a day to maintain troops in Siachen and another two crore a day on the armed forces in Jammu & Kashmir.

The army has also incurred an additional expense of around thirteen hundred crore to equip soldiers for the LoC with high altitude gear. Expensive unattended ground sensors, surveillance radar and secure communication and signal systems will be extra. "The perennial troop deployment in the region will bleed India financially besides tying down a large number of its soldiers in inhospitable conditions," said a senior military officer.

Opting for a "troop-intensive" alternative on the LoC, instead of the more sensible and less expensive mix of partial deployment supplemented by surveillance aids, the army is furiously battling the logistics of building posts before winter sets in around end-September, when movement is possible only by helicopter. These posts will be located every three to five km along the icy stretch, traversed by steep ridges and glacial valleys to house a complement of around twenty-five soldiers each. Engineers are carving out dirt tracks along sheer, rocky mountain faces for porters and mules to ferry material to build insulated shacks before bringing up supplies, especially fuel, for the eight months that the area is cut off. "The resources of India's 1.2-million-strong army will now be stretched not only in manpower but also financially in Kashmir's border-management plans," said a senior military officer involved in the reorganisation. The new front in Kargil that needs constant supervision, alongside counter-insurgency (CI) deployment across Jammu & Kashmir, will require an entirely new strategy, he said, greatly attenuating the army's resources and resilience.

To achieve this the army has raised a new corps of around fifty thousand soldiers and officers to man the LoC in the Kargil region — more than double the pre-Kargil war strength. The new XIV corps will comprise the existing 3 Infantry Division based at Leh bordering Tibet and the 8 Mountain Division with headquarters at nearby Nimu. Both divisions were involved in the Kargil conflict. Till the Kargil war, the defence of the entire state including Siachen was handled by XV corps from its headquarters at Srinagar while Jammu, Poonch and Rajouri in the plains, bordering Pakistan, were the responsibility of XVI corps based at Udhampur, around 120 km to the south.

The reorganisation became necessary after the border war, as XV corps have always found it difficult to man areas east of the thirteen thousand feet high Zojila Pass which are snowbound for seven months every year, completely cutting off the Kargil-Leh region. The absence of a permanent force in the area was one of the principal reasons for the infiltration by Pakistan. Besides, XV corps was also preoccupied with CI Operations (CI Ops). The army has also decided to induct a new division to replace 8 Mountain Division at Sharifabad, near Srinagar, which was combating militancy before being moved to Kargil in May. This new force will supplement the division-strong Rashtriya Rifles, a "dedicated" army counter-insurgency unit which has been fighting Kashmiri militants since its raising in the early 1990s.

A Dismal Failure

But other than braving the cold, the soldiers will also have to run the gauntlet of Pakistani mortars and artillery guns as the entire region along the LoC has been marked by Pakistan, making Indian soldiers sitting targets. "The Indian posts will have to be cleverly sited to evade Pakistani artillery," said one officer. Some military-planners have recommended a "circumspect" and economical approach to manning the LoC by raising an additional force of Ladakh Scouts, the locally recruited militia which fought valiantly alongside the Indian Army to evict the intruders, and tasking them with the frontier's security. The proposal is reportedly under "consideration".

Intelligence officials said Pakistani deployment along the LoC, on the other hand, would be a fraction of India's, as Islamabad was confident that New Delhi would not transgress the frontier. Pakistan had the added advantage of a landing strip in Gultari in Pakistan-administered Kashmir for short-takeoff and landing (STOL) aircraft. The Pakistani Army also had roads running from Gultari, the nearby military township of Skardu and adjoining Olithingthang to points near the LoC.

There is enough evidence that the army ignored reports and obvious indicators about the imminence of the Pakistani intrusion. Even National Security Adviser Brajesh Mishra admitted that India had been "surprised" by Pakistan in Kargil. Official sources said that though the overall intelligence apparatus failed miserably, there was still enough intelligence provided to 3 Infantry Division responsible for the LoC. But its senior commanders failed to anticipate the Pakistani invasion, and to gauge its intensity almost three weeks after it was discovered.

So utterly confident was 3 Infantry Division — despite its dedicated intelligence wing — of the fact that Pakistan posed no danger, that it even diverted 70 Infantry Brigade stationed at

Batalik to the Kashmir Valley in February 1998 on counter-insurgency operations — the preoccupation of the military's higher command. This left the Batalik sub-sector relatively unprotected and ultimately accounted for the deep intrusions. "It was a complete lack of threat assessment and failure of surveillance by 3 Infantry Division at the higher command level," said a senior officer. All intelligence, he said, was viewed piecemeal and little or no attempt was made to collate it. Doing so would have revealed Pakistan's bigger game plan of occupying the ridges in order to interdict Highway 1 A by directing artillery fire onto it.

In August 1998 locals from Yaldor village in the Batalik region close to the LoC had reportedly informed 3 Infantry Division about sixteen Pakistanis who visited them, seeking information about Indian troop deployment in the region. The Division was also provided intelligence about Pakistan building an all-weather road from Gultari (along which its army eventually pushed its supply convoys and artillery pieces to the front during the border war which were responsible for the majority of Indian casualties). "It was no great secret that Pakistan had been building a road in the region since 1997 or amassing troops of the NLI at Skardu," said a civilian intelligence source. He said the Division either blatantly ignored reports of repeated incursions by Pakistani helicopters and unmanned aerial vehicles (UAVs) into its area of responsibility or was simply unable to comprehend their import.

The army was also reportedly forwarded a report in the December 1998 issue of *Al Dawa,* a monthly magazine published by the Lashkar-e-Taiba militant group based at Lahore, that the predominantly Afghan militant group had successfully pushed some of its cadres into the Kashmir Valley through the Drass region. *Al Dawa* declared that the militants were trained at Skardu, headquarters of Pakistan's 62 and 80 Brigades that are part of the

A Dismal Failure

Force Commander Northern Area (FCNA) with headquarters at Astor. And March onwards, local Urdu papers across Pakistan also carried frequent reports about the successful incursion by its army and mercenaries into Indian Kashmir.

Around mid-March, some two months before the intrusions were incidentally confirmed by some shepherds, two separate patrols by men of the 3 Punjab Battalion fired on at least two different groups of around six to eight armed men "dressed in black" in the Batalik region near the LoC, before they managed to slip away. The patrol leaders reportedly informed their unit commanders who in turn are believed not to have passed on the intelligence of the encounter to 121 Brigade headquarters at Kargil tasked with manning the LoC. "In hindsight, it seems that the intruders slipped away to their hideouts and bunkers well inside Indian territory unknown to the Indian Army," one officer said. According to war diaries of Pakistani officers recovered from Batalik, Drass and Mushkoh, the phased intrusion by the NLI began around mid-February and continued well into March.

The NLI operating under FCNA was raised in 1973 from locally recruited militias like the Karakoram, Gilgit and Northern Scouts. Trained in mountain warfare, its seventeen battalions specialise in heli-borne, commando operations. Army officers said the NLI's capabilities include seizing and holding ground and conducting independent operations in varied climatic conditions of the type executed in Kashmir.

Eleven days after the army admitted its first patrol was ambushed along the LoC in Kargil by Pakistani soldiers on 8 May, Lt. General Krishan Pal, commander of XV corps incharge of the region, claimed there were no "battle indicators of war or even limited skirmishes." On 19 May General Pal, security adviser to the Kashmir government, told the Unified Headquarters (UHQ) meeting at Srinagar that there "was no concentration of troops on the Pakistani side." The UHQ is Kashmir's topmost security organisation involving the military and civilian establishments, including intelligence agencies, and was established in 1990 to deal with the state's armed separatist movement.

According to the minutes of the UHQ meeting, attended amongst others by the state's chief minister, Farooq Abdullah, senior bureaucrats, high-ranking paramilitary personnel and local intelligence officials, General Pal declared the "situation (in Kargil) was local and would be defeated locally." He said the army convoys were moving "unhindered" in the area and that the civil convoys would commence "soon."

Around the same time General Pal said in an interview that even if he ignored the intruders it would make no difference. "If they come off (the heights) in the summer they will be slaughtered. And if they don't leave them in the winter they will freeze to death," General Pal told *Frontline* magazine, blissfully oblivious to the deathly situation already in place. Subsequent reports, however, place the level of intrusion at its peak at nearly two brigades or around four thousand to five thousand soldiers from the NLI alongside the locally raised Chitral and Gilgit Scouts and some Islamic mercenaries and half that number at its lowest level towards the end of the fighting in July.

Senior officers said General Pal's faulty judgement and failure to correctly assess the situation led to complacency amongst the senior commanders. This, in turn, led to the Northern Army commander and overall incharge of the operation, Lt. General H.M. Khanna's lop-sided and inaccurate briefing of Defence Minister George Fernandes. Consequently, the minister declared in May that the infiltrators would be "flushed out" within forty-eight hours.

A Dismal Failure

"The responsibility of the higher command is not to lead men into battle but to make accurate assessments and to act on them professionally," said one officer. The bravery of the soldiers and young officers who fought valiantly bailed out their senior commander's collective incompetence, he said. It was unlikely, he added, that any of the senior officers

The ordinary jawan as well as the officers who fought the Kargil war would like heads to roll but this is unlikely to happen.

would be held accountable for waging war to recapture India's own territory, securely held by Pakistan for several months. And though the government had instituted an inquiry into the fiasco, few in the army were optimistic that it would fix accountability for the intelligence and military lapses.

The inquiry committee that included two National Security Council advisory board members — K. Subrahmanyam and B.G. Verghese — and Lt. General K.K. Hazari, former vice chief of army staff, had neither the authority nor the jurisdiction to summon witnesses or demand classified reports to help them get a clear picture of the border conflict. This would hamper them in pinpointing the overall intelligence failure. Analysts have dismissed the inquiry as a "gimmick" by the BJP-led caretaker government ahead of the general elections.

"Hiding behind the grit and bravery of the units that successfully vacated the Pakistani intrusion, the senior army establishment has cleverly begun deflecting attention from the basic question of why such a massive military operation was necessary in the first place," said one army officer. It was unlikely, he said, that any of the senior officers, including division and corps commanders, would be held accountable for the lapse.

Officers and jawans who participated in the operations have resigned themselves to the inevitable — that the accountability process will be overshadowed by the euphoria over their achievements against impossible odds. "Heads should roll, but little will happen," said several officers, all declining to be named.

Military sources said the army's quiet "cover-up" had already started. They said Brigadier Surinder Singh, commander of the independent 121 Brigade based at Kargil in whose area of responsibility a large proportion of the intrusions took place, had informed his superiors, including the chief of army staff, General

A Dismal Failure

V.P. Malik, of the impending invasion but was ignored. Of course, this does not absolve Brigadier Singh of blame for the Kargil failure. The army, for its part, accuses Brigadier Singh of lying and claims he provided no warning.

Few know that General Malik (behind Vajpayee) usurped the role of Lt. General Khanna, who was technically incharge of Kargil operations.

Military officers have also questioned General Malik usurping the role of the Northern Army Commander Lt. General H.M. Khanna, head of Operation Vijay, as the exercise to push back the Kargil intruders was named. General Malik, who did not deem it fit to cancel his ten-day-long trip to Eastern Europe in mid-May, despite being fully aware of the intrusion, took charge of Operation Vijay only after returning home. He visited Srinagar and Kargil on at least five occasions, accompanying both the prime minister and the defence minister.

Few even know that in the army's operational hierarchy it was General Khanna's responsibility to conduct operations in Kargil. "As it turned out, General Khanna's role was notional," said one officer. "Discarding the chain of command General Malik so assiduously advocates," he said, "the army chief opted to override his commander and conduct the operations himself."

In a belated attempt at explaining away the intrusion, General Malik told newsmen that the army's surveillance and radar capabilities were poor as it was inadequately equipped. He is probably unaware that nearly six years ago the army was solely responsible for rejecting, for inexplicable and mysterious reasons, a battle-field surveillance radar (BSR) whose purchase it had earlier cleared. The lack of a BSR has now become one of the army's many alibis for the intelligence failure in Kargil.

The civilian intelligence apparatus too failed miserably. Army sources said India's counter-intelligence organisation, the Research and Intelligence Wing or RAW, provided no information on the troop build-up and activity across the LoC in Pakistan despite abundant resources. They said its Aviation Research Centre (ARC) never carried out routine recces with its sophisticated Electronic Intelligence (Elint) aircraft between January and April nor were its overseas operatives aware that Pakistan had bought over fifty thousand pairs of snow boots and winter clothing from European manufacturers. When India went shopping for them across Europe in May and June, stocks of high-altitude clothing and boots had reportedly run out.

A Dismal Failure

Army officers said the rivalry between civilian and military intelligence led RAW to rarely provide the army with "decent" intelligence even though a majority of its information concerned military affairs. Senior military officers said most RAW operatives, recruited mainly from the police, were also not familiar with military matters and hence incapable of providing accurate information on defence-related issues.

The army has also disputed the effectiveness of air strikes carried out over nearly six weeks. Field commanders said the proficiency of over five hundred attack sorties against Pakistan intruders was "limited," significantly less than the claims made by senior IAF officials in New Delhi. "The hit rate of the air force was in inverse proportion to their sincerity in participating in the Kargil campaign," said an army officer in Drass. He said for nearly three weeks after the air strikes began on 26 May their effectiveness was "insufficient."

In addition to losing two MiG series fighters and one Mi 17 helicopter gun ship on two successive days, in an environment the IAF monopolised, the air force simply failed in destroying Pakistani sangars (rock bunkers) or dislodging the intruders in any significant way. "They (the air force) were unable to dominate the terrain and the high mountain ranges," said an army officer. They managed limited combat effectiveness flying around five km above the minuscule targets and releasing their ordnance at "safe heights."

At one point early on in the conflict, the army reportedly asked the IAF to call off its air strikes which were not only proving ineffective, but also posing a threat to troops ascending hillsides. Often army units advantageously poised were forced to halt or postpone their advance in deference to air strikes which frequently never materialised due to the sudden advent of clouds, common in the region, forcing troops to retreat, regroup and launch a fresh offensive, taking heavy casualties. "If the air force had been an effective force multiplier, these delays in moving forward would have been acceptable," said one officer. "Since they were not, they were an irritant." Even General Malik told *Sunday* magazine in an interview that "air (strikes) were not as effective against enemy posts but the IAF kept innovating and were ever willing."

This situation reportedly led to the chief of air staff, Air Marshal A.Y. Tipnis, rushing to XV corps headquarters midway through the conflict and conferring with the army commanders to work out new strategies. Thereafter, Mirage 2000 fighters, amongst the most sophisticated in the IAF's inventory, were seriously pressed into service, firing locally-designed laser-guided bombs with relatively greater proficiency.

Earlier, in May, when the extent, depth and seriousness of Pakistani intrusions was discovered, the IAF is believed to have sidestepped requests by the army to attack the infiltrators. They claimed inexperience in mountain warfare, terrain unfamiliarity and inadequate hardware to undertake the task. This led to Prime Minister Atal Behari Vajpayee assuring Pakistan that no air strikes would be undertaken. A few days later, the IAF were presented with a *fait accompli* and pressed into attack on 26 May. After losing three aircraft in as many days the IAF panicked, changed tack and began operating from a "safe" distance.

For the first two days of air strikes, Mi 17 air force pilots attacking intruder bases carried an officer of the Army Aviation Corps (AAC) aboard as a guide. AAC pilots operate daily in the area, dropping supplies and evacuating casualties and are thoroughly familiar with the terrain. On 28 May when the Mi 17 was shot down by a shoulder-held Stinger missile, no AAC pilot was aboard.

Officials said the other mismatch between the army and the IAF was in precisely pinpointing targets. While the army's C3I (Command, Control, Communication and Intelligence) system was digitised, the IAF's Air Defence Ground Environment System was not. And while conversions were elementary, the slightest error in calculation would lead to a wide miss on the ground. "A miss by a few yards where precision is vital, is as good as a few miles," said an army officer.

Also, the IAF's array of weapons is configured for use at sea level. Having never operated at such heights, few pilots in the IAF could accurately estimate their trajectories, resulting in rockets and other precision-guided munitions smashing harmlessly into the mountain side. These misses did not reportedly improve with mission frequency a few days before the conflict ended. Senior IAF officials, however, have gone to extraordinary lengths to prove their force's proficiency through detailed briefings and pictures, a view not shared by troops on the ground. But there remains little doubt that the IAF did create a world record operating at the heights it did, battling terrific odds in relatively outdated aircraft and providing a tactical, psychological edge to the army over the Pakistani invaders.

The rivalry between the army and the air force for supremacy has plagued military planners for decades. Heated debate has centred around the issue of unified command which the IAF has resisted, believing that air assets should never be parcelled out. The IAF doctrine states that the fight for "control of the air should get first priority in every case." "The fight between the two over operational matters has never been resolved," said a senior officer.

Analysts say that in the event of a war with Pakistan, the IAF wants to fight a strategic air battle aiming at economic targets (oil refineries, railways, etc), destroying the enemy's war-waging capability. But going by past experience, no such war can last more than ten to twelve days (neither side has the resources to sustain it beyond that), during which it would be impossible to factor in a strategic air battle. Military planners said the IAF was also wary of operating in tactical battle areas, preferring instead the safer option of "interdicting" operations. "The IAF has not trained itself for close support tasks with the army," said a senior officer. He also said the IAF had persistently denied the army attack helicopters, operating which would have proven highly effective against the Pakistani intruders.

The conflict in Kashmir was the first military showdown between the neighbours since both became nuclear weapon states and began building missiles to strike deep into each other's territory. Two of their wars have been over Kashmir and India accuses Pakistan — an allegation it denies — of "sponsoring" Islamic insurgents fighting a civil war for an independent Muslim homeland since 1989. Last year's nuclear tests by the two arch rivals only worsened the "no war, no peace" situation between the two neighbours in which they routinely exchange thousands of rounds of artillery, mortar and machine gun fire daily along extended portions of the LoC. India claims fire from the Pakistani side is cover for the infiltration of armed militants into the state. Pakistan says it is defensive fire in response to India's belligerence.

"Possession of nuclear weapons has emboldened Pakistan to raise the military stakes at a time and place of its choosing," said a military officer. The weapons of mass destruction offered Pakistan an opportunity to force a military conflict in Kashmir, he said, that ensured international intervention in the dispute whenever fears of an escalation loomed and the spectre of a nuclear weapon exchange appeared imminent. "In its posturing Pakistan has just one rung of escalation — from low to medium intensity conflict to the nuclear option," the officer said, making South Asia one of the world's major flash points.

Security analysts believe Pakistan will continue to push India, ensuring that it does not drive it across its threshold of tolerance. Lt. General Javed Nasir, formerly of the ISI, agrees. "India could enlarge the situation prior to 28 May (when Pakistan carried out its nuclear tests)," he states in a recent issue of *Pakistan's Defence Journal*. It dare not do so now, not even in "hot pursuit." Pakistani military planners realised that weapons of mass destruction presented them an opportunity to force a limited, conventional war in Kashmir whenever it wanted and began seriously preparing for the Kargil intrusion.

They reasoned, and rightly so, that such a military engagement — the first ever between two nuclear powers — would ensure international attention. The Indian government, for its part, had doggedly refused to even consider the possibility of a "window" of conventional conflict existing in a nuclear environment. It reasoned that nuclear deterrence and the prospect of mutually assured destruction (MAD) in the event of a nuclear exchange would bring peace to a turbulent region. "To have factored in this possibility of a limited military engagement would merely have conceded the absurdity of the BJP-led government's flawed politics," said a military official.

Kashmir's continuing insurgency has imposed another burden on the over-extended army and one it is ill-equipped to handle. Till the mid-1990s, infantry battalions assigned to CI Ops for two years were assured a three-year peace tenure thereafter. But with the armed rebellion nowhere close to ending, peacetime duty tours of infantry troops had decreased to around two years, leave was infrequent and indiscipline had multiplied.

"Those fighting insurgencies remain under constant tension 24 hours a day and 365 days a year," wrote Lt. General Nasir in *Pakistan's Defence Journal* recently. The insurgents can strike anywhere, anytime leading to short tempers and frustration, stated the former head of the counter-intelligence agency that successfully ran the Afghan mujahideen or freedom fighters against the Soviets occupying Afghanistan in the 1980s.

Many infantry units which had done at least two and even three CI duty tours in Kashmir, were presently being readied for yet another or alternately being deployed further north in Kargil. Military officials conceded such frequent CI deployments had led to mental breakdowns and several instances of "fragging" in which soldiers reeling under unrelenting pressure by competitive battalion commanders to swiftly produce results, had shot dead their comrades before killing themselves.

"In CI Ops the biggest challenge a field commander faces is constantly motivating his men to fight a war within the country," said Lt. General V.K. Nayar, former Western Army commander and a low intensity conflict expert. The shortage of around fourteen thousand officers, mostly captains and majors, also had an adverse impact on the combat performance of battalions in Kashmir. Officials said frontline units often operated with less than half their sanctioned strength of officers.

To relieve the pressure on overburdened infantry battalions, soldiers from artillery, mechanised infantry and even armoured units had been deployed on CI Ops after "mothballing" their equipment. Many of these units, however, had recently returned to the plains as fears increased of the Kargil conflict escalating.

A Dismal Failure

The two sides have moved their armies closer to the border in Punjab and neighbouring Jammu and the contiguous desert region of Rajasthan and Sindh provinces in India and Pakistan respectively in readiness for battle, besides cancelling leave for all military personnel.

Since 1990 the army had killed around 8,300 militants in encounters and apprehended another twenty-four thousand till June 1999. Another eighteen hundred had surrendered with their weapons. Arms recoveries for the same period included 19,199 assault rifles, mostly AK 47s, 1,054 machine guns, 1,181 rocket launchers, 288 sniper rifles and one anti-aircraft gun. The army also recovered 4,939 anti-personnel and anti-tank mines, four missile launchers, and 29 mortars. Other seizures included 20,157 kg of explosives and 3,043 improvised explosive devices (IEDs) responsible for the army's mounting casualty rate over the past five years.

Pakistan has never forgiven India for splitting it in two by creating Bangladesh. Besides, Kashmir also remains the "unfinished business" of Partition for Pakistan. It accuses India of reneging on its promise of holding the UN-sponsored plebiscite and insists on third-party mediation to settle Kashmir. Intelligence officials estimate Pakistan spends around two crore a month or twenty-four crore annually to sustain Kashmir's militancy. India's daily expenditure on CI Ops, however, is around two crore a day or around Rs 730 crore per year, around thirty times the amount expended by Pakistan to execute its "death by a thousands cuts" Kashmir policy, by gradually bleeding its neighbour in financial and manpower resources. Delhi spends another three crore a day maintaining troops along Siachen where it daily trades artillery fire with Pakistan and where Indian fatalities due to the inclement weather are heavy. The unofficial estimates of India's expenditure on Kashmir's CI Ops and in Siachen are higher.

According to intelligence estimates there are anywhere between fifteen hundred to two thousand armed mercenaries inside Kashmir — mostly Afghans and Pakistanis — waiting to strike. Consequently, the handful of local militants who remain are feeling the pinch in terms of financial and material support from the ISI and are antagonistic towards the foreigners, whom they also fear. The ISI had also declared that once a foreign militant entered an area, he would automatically assume all operational responsibility for militant operations. This has resulted in instances when disgruntled elements amongst local militants have deliberately led the outsiders into ambushes.

Disparity in militants' allowances had also led to resentment. Intelligence officials said a "foreign" militant received a contract of around two lakh, at least ten times more than what the local was paid. Should the former die in an encounter, his family received insurance of around two to three lakh from the ISI. The family of his Kashmiri equivalent got either a pittance or nothing. The ISI also paid a bonus for killing soldiers, particularly officers, and for massacres that attracted international publicity.

The army, however, does not favour being involved in long internal operations. "The task of counter-insurgency operations is part of our charter because we are committed to fighting for national and territorial integrity," General Malik has said, adding that it is not correct for any army to get over-involved in tackling insurgency operations inside the country. The army chief warned that excessive use of the army against its own people was good neither for the army nor the country and may have an adverse result. But with the Kargil crisis erupting and the potential for similar intrusions in future the army is denied the luxury of choice.

A Dismal Failure

Not wanting to be left out of the action the Indian Navy claimed that strategic manoeuvres by it in the Arabian Sea along Pakistan's coastline hastened the end of the Kargil conflict.

A navy official said three-dimensional battle groups, including frigates, destroyers and submarines from both the Western and Eastern fleets, were deployed off the Pakistani coast, "minutes away" from striking at Karachi harbour, through which over ninety percent of Pakistan's trade, especially its oil supplies, pass. Sea Harrier fighters were positioned to take off from "alternative platforms" like hastily modified tankers in the absence of INS Viraat, the aircraft carrier undergoing a refit at Cochin. Amphibious units of the army and the navy were also moved in from India's Andaman Island chain off the east coast in preparation of a seaborne landing, in case the border war escalated.

"Karachi is Pakistan's jugular vein and we were poised to choke it," said a senior navy officer. "The navy wanted to seize the initiative in case the border conflict intensified," he stated. Strangulation at sea, he added, is slow but deadly and realising this Pakistan signed an agreement in Washington to withdraw the intruders. He said the Indian Navy, with forty-two surface combatants, seventeen submarines and an aircraft carrier, was "preponderant" over the Pakistani Navy, which had six frigates, two destroyers and seven submarines.

Pakistan had put its navy and air force on "high alert" around 28 May, two days after India launched air strikes against Pakistani soldiers and Islamic mercenaries along the LoC. It had also recalled retired air force personnel, shut down its air force training academies and deployed its naval assets including submarines and surveillance aircraft in the area.

The Indian Navy reacted immediately by bringing the Eastern

Fleet to join the Western one in the Arabian Sea, mobilised its surveillance aircraft and began exercising close to the Pakistani coastline. "The navy's objective was conflict prevention through deterrence by showing Pakistan a massive naval build-up," said a senior navy officer. When faced with an adversary whose actions are abnormal and strange, high vigil has to be maintained, he added.

The Indian Navy's Dornier 228 squadron dedicated to information warfare was also deployed during the Kargil operations to assist the army and IAF while sophisticated marine survey equipment was utilised by them to help the air force establish precise co-ordinates and pinpoint targets at heights above fifteen thousand feet.

The media too played the role of a force multiplier during the Kargil conflict. Whilst fighting was still in progress the military demanded nothing other than unquestioning praise for its operations, describing all inquiries into what led to the "near-war" as "untimely" and "anti-national." The army requested circumspection from journalists during the arduous operations and, without exception, was given it.

But with the fighting now over, the army's attitude towards the media has hardened. The army headquarters in Delhi, desperate to whitewash its abysmal failure in discovering the Pakistani intrusions for months on end due to carelessness and complacency, has blocked reporters' access to all field officers other than division commanders.

"The military bureaucrats are anxious to keep all journalists away from media-friendly field soldiers," said an officer. They simply do not want journalists exposed to the anger and sense of betrayal junior officers and jawans feel towards the senior commanders for needlessly placing them in a situation where hundreds of them were killed and wounded. "The army commanders want only adulation from the media," said an officer.

A Dismal Failure

They want no questioning, criticism or blame for the Kargil fiasco, he added.

The real test of any army's ability rests on the manner in which it manages emergencies of the kind that Kargil presented. Sadly, the hierarchy of the military establishment failed to rival the bravery of the junior officers and jawans who eventually saved their senior commanders and India's honour and territorial integrity. What is needed now is introspection and accountability, not empty rhetoric tomtoming victory.

BLUNDERING THROUGH

■ LT. GEN. MOTI DAR

> The former vice chief of army staff questions India's "restraint" in not crossing the LoC during the Kargil war, arguing that militrary considerations must override diplomatic and political compulsions in such situations.

Blundering Through

There is a saying, "War is the mother of lies," and there is yet another saying, "Truth is the first casualty of war." These two sayings have been amply illustrated during the recent Kargil war — a war that should never have happened. However, as war did take place and it captivated the entire nation for two months, there is a need to assess it objectively and to get to the truth even if, like peeling an onion layer by layer, it takes time to get to the core.

Unfortunately, because of the general elections in the country, there was a perceptible slide from nationalism to jingoism and all critical discussion on political and military causes of the war, the accountability of the government, intelligence agencies and the defence services was sought to be silenced by the injunction that no one should belittle the sacrifices of the "heroes of Kargil." Thus an impression was created by the government and some parties that anyone who was critical of the conduct of the war was anti-national. The services too consider criticism of their organisation and leadership as "not in good taste." Thus both the government and the services have built a halo around themselves, which they hope will be reinforced by the three-man committee which is reviewing the war. However, as Captain Liddell Hart, a brilliant strategist and author of *Indirect Approach*, has said, "Whoever habitually suppresses the truth, will produce a deformity from the womb of his thought..." and that "the growth of public criticism is a healthy one — evidence of vitality, not of despondency." Therefore, if we have to see vibrant national foreign and defence policies emerge after Kargil, then we must analyse the Kargil war in depth — fearlessly and objectively. Flaunting patriotism is hardly a substitute for a balanced, realistic and objective appraisal of the war.

That there was an intelligence failure is obvious, as the government and the army were both taken by surprise over the intrusions. All the intelligence agencies — RAW, IB, the army and the BSF as well as the provincial units — failed to provide a clear picture of the Pakistani build-up. There was concentration along the LoC of almost four thousand personnel alongwith their weapons, and fire and logistical support systems. In such rugged terrain such a build-up takes months. Even fragmentary information of movement of troops, training camps, development of roads, tracks and helipads, movement of ponies and porters, build-up of defences, visits of VIPs, air activities, wireless intercepts, etc., should have raised the hackles of the government and of every commander down the line. In other words, if we were alert and inquisitive we ought to have got indications of the build-up, unless the deception plan of Pakistan was exceptionaly brilliant.

Unfortunately, most of the intelligence agencies generally give vague, repetitive and unprocessed information, which cannot be called intelligence. Like earlier wars, well processed and analysed intelligence seems to have been at a premium even in this conflict. In future, therefore, every attempt must be made to coordinate all intelligence systems (from satellite imagery, air reconnaissance, remote-controlled vehicles reconnaissance, wireless interceptions, electronic sensors to human agencies). All the intelligence agencies handling these systems also must coordinate better to provide the defence services and the government a fairly comprehensive picture. The present Joint Intelligence Committe (JIC) is not adequately structured to deal with this and what the defence services need is an equivalent of the Defence Intelligence Agency (DIA), an organisation which the US forces possess and which closely interacts with the CIA and possibly the FBI.

In war, there will never be a complete picture of what is happening on the "other side of the hill" available to the government

Blundering Through

The military leadership seemed to let the political euphoria generated by 'bus diplomacy' cloud its assessment of Pakistani intentions.

or the services. They say, "Intelligence is like an iceberg, only one-third can be seen, while two-thirds is submerged under the water." It takes a sharp intellect to visualise and trace out the form of the submerged iceberg. Obviously, such visualsation did not take place, or else our ship would not have hit the iceberg. One of the things which the Kargil war will be most remembered for is that political euphoria created by "bus diplomacy" seems to have clouded everybody's judgement and instead of questioning and doubting the Pakistani intentions, Indian leaders got carried away and seemed to have dismissed impending threats from their mind. Prime Minister Atal Behari Vajpayee's calling the intrusion a betrayal by Pakistan testifies to such a perception. The higher military leadership also seemed to have got carried away by political assessments and might have concluded that Pakistan had no aggressive intentions. Such misreadings are not new in history — Lord Chamberlain and Stalin had both misread Hitler's aims and intentions. However, what amazes one is the lack of moral courage on the part of both the political and military leadership to accept that besides inadequate intelligence, it was their own assessment which went wrong. It is not clear why even the army, which always has its ears to the ground, was unable to appreciate the impending threat realistically.

The troops on the ground are never adequate to hold the entire length of LoC, especially in the Kargil sector which stretches approximately 150 km. The deployments are made based on likely routes of ingress along the valleys, with the shoulders of the valleys being strongly held. The gaps between the main positions are covered with lighter deployment and surveillance elements. There are reconnaissance patrols, strong standing patrols, link patrols, observations posts, ambushes, and long range patrols to keep surveillance of the gaps. Reserves are kept to deal with any infiltration or intrusion. In Kargil, where the terrain is very rugged and barren, there are severe problems of movement of troops and holding of certain heavy snow-bound areas but with an advantage that the visibility (except in bad weather) is very good and surveillance can be carried out effectively. Besides this, satellite images, air photographs and helicopter reconnaissance are made available from time to time, and there is also effective wireless interception of the enemy's electronic means. The local population of Kargil (comprising of Shias, Buddhists and some Sunni Muslims) have been loyal and friendly and have had very close interaction with army. In war as well as peace they have provided the army and its agencies excellent information about all unusual movements, ingress and intrusion into our territory. Why surveillance failed in this sector this time round is a matter of serious investigation.

Once the intrusions of the Pakistani troops and militants were discovered, the government and the army made many initial blunders. Defence Minister George Fernandes declared that the intruders would be thrown out in forty-eight hours, while the army kept reacting to the intrusions piecemeal and in haste. They sent forward a small body of troops without adequate preparations and with plans which were not well-coordinated. Without adequate information and insufficient artillery or air support, these troops were beaten back with heavy casualties. The government, the army and the nation were bewildered and disoriented for almost twenty days before a cohesive response in terms of air attacks, proper build-up of troops, fire support means and logistics was in place and well-coordinated attacks could be launched. Simultaneously, the government also swung into action on the diplomatic front to retrieve the situation.

The major decision that needed to be made was whether to cross the LoC so as to threaten Pakistani lines of communication, administrative build-up and communication and control centres or to fight the battle on our own side of the LoC. This is what Captain Liddell Hart has to say, "... in the face of the overwhelming evidence of history, no general is justified in launching his troops to a direct attack on an enemy firmly in position." Militarily it made sense to cross the LoC but politically it was decided to restrict operations to our side of the LoC and tell the world that we were restraining ourselves so as to prevent escalation of the

Moti Dar

Was it justified to exercise restraint and not cross the LoC just to please the international community?

war and the prospect of a nuclear confrontation. Was this political decision justified? Some of the issues which need to be debated are:

— Are we to assume that any nation whose borders have been violated, instead of opting to fight for what is militarily advantageous, opts to restrict its operations to its own areas even at considerable human cost, only to please the international community? Much has been made by the government and the media about the virtues of "restraint." But Pakistan did not respect the LoC, so why should we have respected it? Which Western nation would have accepted the violation its of its borders and not carried the war into enemy territory? The US and NATO did not restrain themselves in Yugoslavia and besides inflicting heavy civilian casualties, they destroyed the entire infrastructure of that country only to ensure that their ground troops did not have to fight and suffer casualties. One also cannot imagine China exercising such "restraint."

— That a direct attack on our side of the LoC on fixed Pakistani positions will cause heavy causalities to our troops is known to every military mind. Are we to accept "body bags" in hundreds while Western powers, who probably advocated and appreciated our "restraint," would not accept a single such "body bag" coming home? As General Patton used to say, he did not want his men to die for his country, he wanted the enemy to do so. In such decisions military plans must override diplomatic requirement. The genius of diplomacy lies in being able to support military decisions and yet get favourable international opinion.

— We have declared from the tree tops that Kashmir is an integral part of India, that any attack on Kashmir is an attack on India and therefore, we reserve the right to strike across the LoC. This was the stand which Lal Bahadur Shastri took in 1965 when he ordered the army to cross the border and carry the battle into Pakistan. Doesn't our stand on Kargil weaken our stand on Kashmir?

— If there are to be "more Kargils" in the future, as some Pakistani leaders have declared, are we to restrain ourselves again to get the backing of the international community, at heavy cost to our troops?

— It is being presumed that had we crossed the LoC, the escalation might have led to a nuclear confrontation. If that was the government's assessment, Pakistan has obviously succeeded in using its nuclear capability to deter us. Should we have not called this bluff, especially with our superior conventional and nuclear capability? Would Pakistan leadership be mad enough to use its nuclear weapon just because we crossed the LoC? They are likely to use the nuclear weapons only when the battle situation becomes so critical and desperate for them that the very existence of their nation is threatened. Somehow we are obsessed with a perception that the Pakistan leadership is prone to acting irrationally. In international affairs brinkmanship exists and in the case of Pakistan it has almost succeeded. Recently, when we unfolded our nuclear doctrine, a large number of Pakistani leaders and intellectuals have logically asserted that it would be futile and costly to get into a nuclear arms race with India and that minimum deterrence is all that they should aim at. This does not show that the Pakistani leadership is irrational.

— Ever since the BJP-led government came to power, it has been talking of a "pro-active" policy on Kashmir, thereby implying that we would take actions to attack Pakistani training camps from where the militants are launched. Pakistan having violated the LoC gave us an opportunity to launch such strikes, even if doing so would have meant using our special forces. By missing this opportunity we have invited massive infiltration of militants into the Valley with serious consequences to follow.

— Were there factors other than our restraint which led the US, the G-8 and the Chinese to back us and stand by India during the Kargil crisis? Yes, there were — it was in their own larger strategic interest that these countries supported India's stand and not only because of our restraint. We shall discuss this issue later in the piece.

It was obvious that once the strategic decision not to cross the LoC was taken, the attacks on Pakistani positions would have to be direct and would result in heavy casualties to Indian troops. These could only be minimised by well-coordinated tactical plans closely supported by accurate artillery and air support. Attacks from unexpected directions and deception should also have been an important part of the plans. As the lines of communication of Pakistani forces and their fire support means could not be tackled without crossing the LoC, it became imperative to put international pressure on Pakistan to withdraw from Kargil, otherwise the battle might have carried into the winter and perhaps even until next summer. It is to the credit of tactical commanders, junior officers and our troops that the plan to recapture the heights dominating our Srinagar-Leh national highway succeeded. The junior officers and troops fought with great grit, determination and courage to capture the most difficult mountain top positions in extremely trying conditions of high altitude. The tactical plans, employment of the artillery and the air support displayed great innovativeness. The courage, valour and the fortitude displayed by officers and troops speaks volumes of motivational level of soldiers and airmen for which both the political and military leaderships deserve great compliments. It was a famous victory for the units which took part in the battle, and they have made a permanent niche for themselves in the annals of Indian military history.

Pakistan, which had got itself into a "no win" situation with unfavourable world opinion against it and we, who had been surprised by the Pakistani intrusion, started looking towards the US to resolve the mess, especially as our elections were round the corner. The US administration was now in a position to manipulate both the countries and also to further their own agenda. There being no "free lunches" in international affairs, what we have had to compromise to get US support will only surface with time. Whether the price will be in terms of signing the Comprehensive Test Ban Trerty, or acceptance of Missile Technology Control Regime or resolving the Kashmir issue is still unclear. The euphoria of the international community being supportive of us has already started fading, with the US critical of our nuclear doctrine as well as our shooting down of Pakistan's Atlantique aircraft. While the minister for external affairs, Jaswant Singh, and his men did a splendid diplomatic job, it is also apparent that the Pakistani pull-back was as much due to the efforts of the attacking troops in Kargil and the strategic pressures that were brought on it by concentrating our forces in sensitive areas along the LoC. However, our large concentrations in the Kargil sector led to the Kashmir Valley becoming vulnerable to heavy infiltration of militants, leading to subsequent flaring up of violence in the Valley. The war also made the people of Kargil, Drass and other areas homeless.

The Kargil war has exposed our weaknesses in this sector, and additional forces will now be required here. But we need to be discerning and only after a realistic appreciation of Pakistani capabilities should we decide upon a minimum essential requirement of troops. The Pakistan-occupied Kashmir (PoK) side of the area is not so well-served with roads and the distances to their main bases are very long. If our intelligence is reasonable, we should be able to tackle operational situations in this sector by holding the main valleys and important heights in strength, while the gaps could be occupied by sufficient surveillance troops, and technical and electronics surveillance systems. We also need to hold strong reserves to reinforce our positions and to tackle any infiltration that may take place. On our own side, we have an excellent Srinagar-Leh highway, but it is closed from mid-

November to mid-June because of heavy snow accummulation on Zojila Pass. The alternative route to Ladakh over Rohtang Pass is also closed for a similar period. This restricts us to building up our entire logistics during the season when roads are open, as air transportation is a costly exercise. It seems, however, that there is already an over-reaction to the just-ended Kargil crisis and that a large body of troops may get inducted, causing heavy drain on the exchequer. The reinforcement of the Kargil sector would also have little effect on the situation in the Valley, which is our major area of concern.

After the Kargil war, there have been very bold assaults on the army and other security forces camps, the likes of which did not take place during the last ten years of insurgency and hence the body-bags continue to come. Pakistan has stepped up its military, political and moral assistance to the militants in the Valley and is urging them to "liberate" the Valley. Their actions are being controlled and coordinated with military precision by the Pakistani Army. The majority of the militants are not local Kashmiris; some of them have fought in Afghanistan. Pakistan also continues to raise the Kashmir issue in all international forums and has been urging the US and China to resolve it. We would be running away from the truth if we were to say that Kargil did not internationalise the Kashmir issue. The US, the G-8 countries and China backed us only because they happened to see the Kargil situation spinning out of control and escalating to a nuclear flash point. Defusing such a situation was high priority for the US. Thus if the government sees the US stand on the Kargil crisis as a major shift in its policy in the region, it is in for disappointment.

The US would like to improve its relations with India, but not at the cost of Pakistan. Although Pakistan has ceased to be a front-line state for the US, it still is important to them because of US interest in Caspian and Central Asian oil, and its desire to have control over Islamic militants in Afghanistan and the Taliban (who have given sanctuary to Osama Bin Laden), as also the fear that nuclear technology may be passed on to other Islamic governments and fundamentalist organisations. The US role in Kargil may have pleased elite opinion in India because of Washington's indirect, three-way mediation in New Delhi's favour. The next time around such mediation may well be unfavourable. It would be self-delusion to believe that a "strong," "responsible" India "commands" attention. It does not correspond to the reality of a still skewed triangular US-India-Pakistan relationship after and despite Kargil. India despite its recent strides in information technology, would remain a small technology source and a minor trade partner with the US and hence the latter would do little to disturb its major trade relationship with China. And China would not like to disturb its relationship with Pakistan, because the latter has the potential for fomenting militancy in the Xinjiang province. China also looks forward to developing a petroleum pipeline from Caspian and Central Asian republics to the Xinjiang province with Pakistan's influence in the region.

Immediately after the 1971 Indo-Pak war, when our overwhelming conventional superiority helped to liberate Bangladesh, Pakistan realised that the only answer to conventional superiority was to develop a nuclear weapon to deter India in future wars. Our testing of nuclear devices emboldened Pakistan to also carry out its own nuclear tests, thus giving its army and political bosses the confidence that in future, they may be able to deter Indian conventional superiority and pull off territorial gains either by use of force or through insurgency. Although the brinkmanship and the gamble did not pay off in

Kargil, the nuclear deterrent has come to stay in the subcontinent.

India has released its nuclear doctrine document and is on its way to weaponisation, putting in place a command and control system and developing delivery means in terms of intermediate range and intercontinental ballistic missiles and submarine-based systems. Pakistan also has similar ambitions, but indications are they may not get into the nuclear arms race considering the serious implications it would have on their already weak economy. We too would be spending a colossal amount of money on the development of nuclear capability, which we can ill-afford at present. A dialogue needs to be initiated between us, China and Pakistan for more rational nuclear policies to emerge.

The Kashmir issue is probably the most incompetently handled political issue since independence. The Indian government has ignored the actual wishes of the Kashmiri people, just as Pakistan has done in the case of PoK. In fact, the government of PoK is much less free than the state government of Jammu & Kashmir ever has been. The Kashmir issue has further been complicated because of the territorial dispute emanating from the geopolitical objectives of the two national states. Siachen and Kargil have been manifestations of such conflicting interests. We have not respected the promises made to the people of Kashmir in 1948 and the resultant resentment has not been assuaged by the subsequent regimes at the Centre. Instead, corrupt state governments in Kashmir have had the backing of the Centre. This has resulted in lack of development, unemployment and political disillusionment in Jammu & Kashmir thus providing a fertile ground for Pakistan to indoctrinate the youth on Islamic fundamentalism and breed insurgency, which flared up in 1989-90. By the summer of 1996, the insurgency had been brought under control to an acceptable level by the army and other security forces and elections to both Lok Sabha and the state assembly were held. Tempers in the Valley cooled down and people started looking forward to peace, stability and economic well-being. However, an ineffective administration failed to develop infrastructure or build the state's economy. Political steps towards reconciliation and displaying sensitivity to people's demand for autonomy were never seriously taken up by the government. Some parties continued to canvas for scrapping of Article 370 thus giving an impression to the people of Kashmir that the Central government was not serious about negotiating an autonomous status for them. The downside towards militancy again started and in fact the ratio of terrorists to securitymen killed came down from 5.8:1 in 1997 to 2:1 by July 1999. Pakistan once again started pushing in the mercenary Afghan, PoK and other Middle East militants. It is in this context that the occupation of territory in Kargil to cut off Ladakh from the Valley took place. Pakistan is likely to step up the insurgency, disturb elections and continue in its pursuit to force international community to accept its aim of having a "plebiscite" or referendum in Jammu & Kashmir. Of late Pakistan has got emboldened by the extremely poor turnout for the elections in the Valley and by the UN referendum in East Timor. We, therefore, have to crush militancy with a heavy hand, while developing confidence among the Kashmiris that we genuinely understand their aspirations of autonomy and would be politically prepared to adjust. Above all, it is the economic well-being of the Kashmiri people which can see us through. Unless the people of Kashmir are with India this proxy war will never be won.

There has been a jingoistic demand that we should do to Pakistan what they have done to us, in other words develop insurgencies with a view to break up Pakistan or to once and for all fight a major war with Pakistan. Such thoughts are fraught with grave danger, because a fragmented Pakistan would be weak and hence a rouge state. The fissiparous tendencies would bounce back on us thus destabilising the region. With nuclear capability in hand, a weak Pakistan government may well endanger the peace and a real nuclear threat may develop. The threat from Pakistan and the pressures from the international community would only recede if we were to develop our economy rapidly and emerge as a strong economic power — everything else could and would follow.

The intrusion in Kargil was a national shame and hence accountability for such a blunder needs to be pinpointed if we are to ensure the security of the nation in future. The negligence has cost the nation approximately five thousand crore, heavy casualties to the troops and above all, a shadow has fallen on the honour of the nation. A commission of inquiry on the lines of the Shimon Agranat Commission which inquired into the failures of the Yom Kippur war needs to be instituted if we are to get to the truth.

A Defining Moment

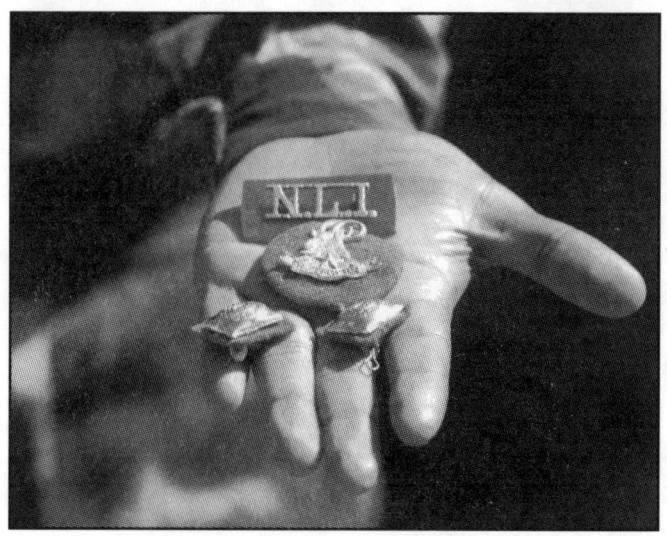

■ J. N. Dixit

India's former foreign secretary on how Pakistan planned and executed the Kargil misadventure, its motivations in doing so, and the lessons for India from this war.

A Defining Moment

Pakistani invasion in the Kargil sector with the active participation of its armed forces has been a defining moment in Indo-Pak relations. It is a catalytic and enlightening event indicating the likely orientations of Indo-Pak relations for the coming decade or two. By this organised military aggression, Pakistan has categorically pulled back from all the commitments which it gave and agreements which it entered into since 1965 and 1972 to resolve the problems affecting Indo-Pak relations and for restoring these relations to some normalcy. The invasion of Kargil is a clear signal that Pakistan considers a hostile and confrontationist relationship with India necessary to serve its national interests. It is in this context that one has to assess and examine the following issues:

What were the motivations of Pakistan in indulging in this military adventurism in Kargil? What was the extent of participation of the Pakistani government in the aggression in the Kargil sector and on the Line of Control (LoC)? What are the lessons that India should learn from the Kargil experience? Should Pakistan be trusted to return to the negotiating table? Should the dialogue be continued? Given the apparent intention of Pakistan to continue its proxy war against India, to destabilise India, how should India deal with this threat? How should India assess the international reaction to the Kargil crisis? What are the lines on which Indo-Pak relations are likely to develop?

Before one proceeds to examine these points, it would be pertinent to describe the geostrategic and demographic characteristics of Kargil and the factual and legal basis of the LoC which divides Pakistan-occupied Kashmir (PoK) from Jammu & Kashmir in India.

Geostrategically, Kargil is a region of undoubted significance for the security of the Kashmir Valley, Ladakh and our military positions on the Siachen glacier. The area lying south and westwards from Ladakh straddles the approaches towards Siachen, Ladakh and the Valley. The area lies within Indian territory east of the LoC and southeast of the Siachen and Saltoro heights which are beyond the northernmost points upto which the LoC has been formally demarcated and delineated (grid reference point NJ-9842). It should be remembered that Kargil is not a part of the valley of Kashmir. It originally was a part of Ladakh, but in recent years has been created into a separate district, because the majority of people living here were Shia Muslims.

Capturing the Kargil area, stretching across 140 km of mountain ranges, would have enabled Pakistan to interdict the highway from the Valley to Ladakh and cut off India's approach both to Ladakh and Siachen. The Kargil sector of the LoC covering the Mushkoh valley, Drass, Kaksar, Chhainikund, Shingo, Batalik and Chorbatla areas, because of the terrain, was not manned in detail and around the year. There were gaps between brigades providing security to the Siachen region and the brigades responsible for security at Kargil and Gurez. But it was felt that the terrain and the Buddhist-Shia population of the area would be a natural preventive factor against any extensive Pakistani military intrusion. Pakistan took advantage of this situation, and regular Pakistani forces came across the LoC all along the 140 km stretch penetrating into Indian territory to a depth of eight to twelve km between March and May 1999. When challenged by India, Pakistan argued that it had not crossed into Indian territory, that the LoC in this sector was not clearly demarcated or delineated. Space does not allow a detailed analysis stressing the validity and legitimacy of the LoC. It would be sufficient to keep the following facts in mind: The LoC is rooted in the cease-fire lines which were drawn up after the 1948 and 1965 wars with Pakistan. The present

LoC was drawn up on the basis of the stipulations of the Simla agreement of July 1972. The line was drawn on the basis of mutual consent between senior army commanders of India and Pakistan. The delineation of the line has been done on nine maps with detailed grid references in the appropriate scale which have been countersigned by military representatives of Pakistan and India. A matter of deliberate significance is that this line was not called a cease-fire line, but a "line of control" (not a "line of actual control," which might have implied that it was a temporary arrangement. This definitely was not the intention. The agreement was for a permanent line.) And this LoC was respected by both sides for a period of twenty-seven years from 1972 to 1999 when Pakistan decided to violate it and question its legitimacy.

What then were the Pakistani motivations in undertaking this patently unprovoked military adventure? The macro level political motivations were: First, the fact that the restoration of an elected government in Jammu & Kashmir and the gradual return of political stability and economic normalcy resulted in Kashmir no longer being seen as area of crisis by the international community. Compounding this situation, from Pakistan's point of view, was the incremental success achieved by the Indian security forces in countering and neutralising Pak-sponsored terrorist activities. The efforts of Pakistan to destabilise and separate Kashmir from India had come to nought. Some effort had to be made, therefore, to refocus international attention on the Kashmir issue within the framework of Pakistani objectives.

Secondly, strategic planners of Pakistan were getting the impression that the international community was incrementally becoming supportive of the idea of a settlement of the Kashmir issue on the basis of some kind of a line of control. So it was decided to change the delineation of the LoC to a more advantageous position in favour of Pakistan. Shifting the LoC eastwards would enable Pakistan to continue its efforts to capture Kashmir from a stronger position.

Thirdly, if this shift of the LoC could be consolidated in the Kargil sector, it would weaken India's strategic capacity to safeguard Ladakh and the Valley. The expectation was that the Chinese would not have minded Pakistan acquiring a more advantageous geostrategic position on the southern and southeastern flanks of the Karakoram highway. If this military conflict engineered by Pakistan could be taken to the threshold of a tangible nuclear confrontation, the international community could be asked to intervene to pressure India to compromise on Kashmir in a manner desired by Pakistan.

Pakistan's overall plans and the detailed military objectives were broadly assessed as follows by the Government of India:

— The plan was to have been kept top secret; the attempt was to involve the least number of people and avoid any activity opposite Kargil which might give away Pakistan's intentions.
— Only an 'in principle' concurrence without any specifics was to be obtained from the Pakistan prime minister.
— A cover plan must exist to obfuscate the aggression and try to bring about defusion of the escalation in an early time frame.
— The operation should help in internationalising the Kashmir issue.

With these terms of reference in mind, the Pakistani Army evolved a plan which was kept confined to the Pakistani Chief of Army Staff (COAS), Chief of General Staff (CGS), Director-General Military Operations (DGMO), GOC 10 Corps and GOC

Force Commander Northern Area (FCNA), who was made overall in charge of operations in the Kargil sector. Even the corps commanders were not kept in the picture. This has been completely substantiated by the taped telephonic conversation between the Pakistani COAS and the CGS.

Pakistan's military aim for carrying out the intrusions was based on the following considerations:

— Exploit large gaps which exist in the defences in the sector both on the Indian and Pakistani sides of the LoC. The terrain is extremely rugged with very few tracks leading from the main roads towards the LoC. During winters, the area gets heavy snowfall making movements almost impossible.
— Zojila Pass normally opens by end May/beginning June, thus moving of reinforcements by road from Srinagar is not possible till then. Pakistan calculated that even if the intrusions were discovered in early May, as it was, the Indian Army reaction would be slow and limited, thereby allowing Pakistan to consolidate the intrusions more effectively. In the event, however, Zojila was opened for troops induction in early May itself.
— The intrusions, if effective, would enable Pakistani troops to secure a number of dominating heights from where the Srinagar-Leh road could be interdicted at a number of places, which was the plan.
— The intrusion would also draw in and tie down Indian reserves.
— The intrusion would alter the status of the LoC, give Pakistan control over a substantial piece of ground across the LoC and enable it to negotiate from a position of strength.

Apart from keeping the plan top-secret, Pakistan decided on the following measures of surprise and deception:
— No induction of any fresh troops into the FCNA for the proposed operation. Any large-scale troop movement (two-three battalions) would have drawn India's attention.
— The artillery which was inducted into the FCNA during the heavy exchange of fire in July-September 1998 was not de-inducted. Since firing continued thereafter, though at a lower scale, this was not considered extraordinary.
— No reserve formations or units were moved into the FCNA till after the execution of the plan.
— The administrative bases for the intrusions were to be catered for from existing defences.
— Logistic lines of communication were to be along the ridge lines and the nullahs well away from the tracks and positions of Indian troops.

The plan, which was simple, was made by creating four independent groups from four infantry battalions and two companies of the Special Service Group which were already located in the FCNA. These were:
— 4 NLI Battalion, the FCNA reserve located in Gilgit.
— 6 NLI Battalion, ex 62 Infantry Brigade located at Skardu.
— 5 NLI Battalion, ex 82 Infantry Brigade located at Minimarg.
— 3 NLI, ex 323 Infantry Brigade located at Dansam.

Special Service Group (SSG): The two companies of SSG were to be broken up into smaller teams of thirty-two to ninety-four among the four battalions.

Additional Resources: The groups were also allotted shoulder-fired Air Defence Missiles of the Stinger variety. This coupled with the 12.7 mm Air Defence (AD) machine guns integral to the NLI Battalions, gave them a modicum of air defence capability.

Use of Militants: Some numbers of militants from Lashkar-e-Taiba, Harkat-ul-Ansar and Afghan war veterans were also grouped with each battalion to give it a facade of jehad. After the intrusion, eight hundred or more militants were brought to Skardu area for further reinforcements.

Artillery Support: Pakistani artillery numbering twenty batteries were to provide fire support to the intruding groups from the Pakistani side of the LoC. This ensured that each intrusion had the support of three to four batteries. Observation post officers from the Pakistani Army were also grouped alongwith line and radio communication.

The plan was put into action towards the end of April. The main groups were broken into a number of smaller sub-groups of thirty to forty each for carrying out multiple intrusions along the ridge lines and occupying dominating heights. The intrusions were in the following four main sub-sectors:

— Batalik   —   250 men (approx.)
— Kaksar   —   100 men (approx.)
— Drass   —   250 men (approx.)
— Mushkoh nullah —   200-300 men (approx.)

Logistics: Logistic support was carried out by soldiers from within each battalion and militants. The route for supply was along ridge lines and nullahs.

Reserves: After the plan had been implemented, Pakistan moved approximately a brigade worth of troops into the FCNA to recreate reserves.

There has been a systematic and consistent effort by the Pakistan government to obfuscate the Kargil issue. As directed by the Pak COAS, the foreign minister of Pakistan, Sartaj Aziz, spoke in different languages without any substance. The shifting stand of Pakistan since then has been on the following lines:

— LoC is delineated but not demarcated. (This is the most brazen attempt towards obfuscation. The line, while not marked on the ground, is clearly identified by both the armies and has remained so for the last twenty-seven years.)
— The Pakistani Army has been in occupation of these heights for a long time.
— The intrusion of the LoC is not by the Pakistani Army but by militants over which Pakistan has no control.
— The Pakistani Army is fighting in Drass and Kargil sectors.

There is ample evidence, therefore, of Pakistan's direct involvement in the invasion of Kargil, notwithstanding much speculative analysis and obfuscatory prognosis on the subject. It is time that India takes note of objective and incontrovertible realities about what Pakistan has been upto and more importantly, have a clear perception of Pakistani motivations on which India should predicate its future policies towards Pakistan.

I personally visited Indian Army establishments where evidence of direct Pakistani military involvement in the conflict was available and was on display. There were arms and ammunition captured from regular Pakistani Army troops with markings and numbers of units to which the weapons belonged. There were a

Captured pay book and identity card (facing page, top) of a Pakistani soldier and Pakistani landmines found in Mushkoh valley.

A Defining Moment

large number of well-thumbed pay books with green covers and relevant official emblems on them of Pakistani military officers and soldiers who were killed in the Kargil battle. There were a sufficient number of operational and battle diaries kept by the Pakistani military personnel. More importantly, the Indian Army now has in its possession battle plans and order of battle directions given to Pakistani field commanders during this conflict which they had noted down in their diaries. There were identity cards, uniforms and relevant military divisional and battalion shoulder patches of Northern Light Infantry and other units of the Pakistani Army taken from dead Pakistani soldiers and officers. The most revealing and poignant of this material were the personal letters written to the soldiers by their family members. Some of them are of such an intimate nature that no civilised armed force or government would give publicity to them. Contents of these letters, mostly written in the Urdu script and local dialects, have been methodically and precisely translated by the Indian Army's intelligence authorities.

The plans for the Kargil invasion were hatched some time in the autumn of 1998 and finalised by January 1999. The intrusion was not a regular, normal, large-scale military phenomenon. It was done gradually over a period of two months, perhaps between March and April 1999. Pakistan primarily relied on troops from the Northern Light Infantry to execute this aggression because soldiers of this regiment are mostly local young men from the mountainous regions of Skardu, PoK, Baltistan, Gilgit and the North West Frontier Province. All of them are fully acclimatised to military activities at high altitudes. They were all ordered to shed their uniforms, put on salwar-kameezes, grow beards and wear skull caps. They were infiltrated in groups of three to four or five to take up positions all across the Kargil sector which they did by the end of April. Their weapons, rations and other items of logistical support were taken across to the positions which they had occupied in a parallel exercise by porters and yaks. The FCNA and the higher command of the 10th Corps of the Pakistani Army provided command and control and full backup support for the military operation. Heavy weapons like mortars, machine guns of various categories and grenade launchers were supplied to their full complement to the soldiers who were ordered to intrude into Indian territories in mufti. Roads and animal paths to carry military supplies were constructed at the maximum heights possible. Helipads were built to back up forward positions taken over by the Pakistani forces in Kargil in the absence of Indian military presence in these areas at that point of time.

An interesting dimension of these Pakistani operations was that the irregulars — barring foreign mercenaries — were used as porters and logistical support personnel by the Pakistani Army. Most of the military operations were carried out by regular Pakistani Army officers and soldiers. Pakistan had also deployed squadrons of its helicopters and its artillery to give cover to the military offensive. General Pervaiz Musharraf, chief of army staff and Lt. General Aziz, chief of general staff of the Pakistani Army Headquarters, were the direct planners and commanding officers of this operation at the highest level. The entire operation was conducted on the basis of full coordination and consensus of the Defence Committee of the Pakistan Cabinet which consists of the prime minister, the foreign minister, the defence minister, the information minister, the home minister and the finance minister, plus the three service chiefs of Pakistan. There is sufficient evidence of this in India's hands, while there is no evidence that the civilian segment of the Pakistan government was averse to this operation. An interesting nuance, however, is that a fair number of corps commanders of the Pakistani Army were not informed of these plans almost till the Indian counter-offensive started. There are reports that General Pervaiz Musharraf and Lt. General Aziz have not been very popular with some of their senior colleagues in recent weeks.

The Pakistani Army units were of course joined by mercenaries from the Afghanistan conflict and by members of the Taliban. The weapons available to the Pakistani aggressors and the logistical support system which they enjoyed alongwith artillery cover and air support nails the lie that Pakistan had no direct involvement in this ill-conceived adventure.

As for the withdrawal from the Kargil sector after 4 July 1999, Pakistan has only withdrawn its regular troops. It has been orchestrating a dispersal of the irregular cadres and so-called mujahideen all along the LoC and into Ladakh and the Kashmir Valley. Regardless of the call for a resumption of dialogue by Pakistan's prime minister Nawaz Sharif and other pretensions, higher levels of violence by Pakistani terrorists inside India is on the cards. While the LoC may be technically respected, Pakistan will continue to exert pressure on it.

The relationship between the two countries is likely to continue to be hostile and confrontationist because of three basic Pakistani motivations which remain unaltered: First, that Pakistan's national consolidation can only be achieved by weakening and fragmenting India. Second, this consolidation cannot be achieved till the territorial aspirations of the Muslim League at the time of Partition, of what Pakistan should have been, are achieved. And third, Pakistan's self-esteem and honour can only be restored if it avenges the defeat of 1971 and the creation of Bangladesh by taking away some territory of India.

A Defining Moment

What are the options for India after the Pakistani withdrawal? Satisfaction tending towards euphoria is characterising Indian reactions both at the governmental and public levels over the "victory" in Kargil. A victory, no doubt, it is, in purely operational military terms, the credit for which goes entirely to our armed forces who fought an extremely difficult campaign in even more difficult terrain. And they did this without having the logical option of a total strategic and military offensive because of the political decision to be restrained and not carry the battle into PoK.

But the point to remember is that this was not a declared war in which India came out successful. It was a counter-offensive in which India succeeded after being initially caught unawares. Whatever explanations and rationalisation we may collectively indulge in about the critical predicament which we faced, there is a need for a thorough and critical introspection about what we have gone through, so that we do not face such a situation again. The second point to remember is that Pakistan agreed to withdraw its intruding forces primarily because of the decisive and determined counter-offensive undertaken by the Indian armed forces. External criticism of Pakistan and the American pressure on it were only secondary factors. Had Pakistan succeeded in its military operations and strategic plans, barring some mild criticism, world powers would not have categorically advised Islamabad to withdraw. They would instead have called for a cease-fire and resumption of dialogue. Pakistan itself would not have succumbed to this external pressure had we allowed it to succeed militarily. External pressure, particularly US pressure, was significant, but basically, it was the Indian military response which brought about the denouement of Pakistani withdrawal.

The third point to remember concerns the two operational

elements in the Clinton-Nawaz Sharif instrument of 4 July in Washington. The relevant elements in the statement are: "They (Clinton and Sharif) also agreed that it was vital for the peace of South Asia that the LoC in Kashmir be respected by both countries in accordance with their 1972 Simla agreement," and, "It was agreed between the President and the Prime Minister that concrete steps will be taken for the restoration of the LoC in accordance with the Simla agreement. The President urged an immediate cessation of hostilities once these steps are taken." It would be pertinent to anticipate the Pakistani interpretations of these two elements in the commitment which Sharif gave Clinton. Both the prime minister and foreign minister of Pakistan as well as Pakistan's military leaders have expressed doubts about the location of the LoC. They have sought discussions on this specific subject, which they will continue to demand. Pakistanis withdrew their troops (only the troops) to their side of the LoC to points where they were before the current conflict occurred, and that only in the Kargil sector. We must remember that the LoC stretches over seven hundred km upto its northern cartographic grid reference point in NJ-9842. The agreement on the LoC states that the line will extend north towards the glaciers without any cartographic details or any ground delineation. There is no formal LoC beyond the ground reference points mentioned above. This portion of the line is called AGPL relating to the location of actual military posts of both countries. Indian positions in Siachen fall in this sector. Pakistan would desire negotiations on the entire LoC with a view to changing its location to their advantage, which we should firmly resist. The Indian demand should be that Pakistani forces pull back to positions which have existed and which have been acknowledged by both sides over the last twenty-seven years, or at least over the last two decades. Furthermore, respecting the

A Defining Moment

LoC and restoration of it within the framework of the Simla agreement should lead to a categorical demand that Pakistan respect its sanctity by withdrawing all secessionist intruders from the Indian side of Jammu & Kashmir, that it should stop all subversive and violent activities in all parts of India and that it dismantle all training camps and training facilities for mercenaries and terrorists within different parts of its own territory, with an additional commitment that it will desist from such activities threatening the territorial integrity of India, as it has agreed to in the Simla agreement (Sub-clauses one to six of paragraph one of the Simla Agreement of 1972).

There are two prospects India can clearly anticipate. First, there would be insistence from Pakistan and pressure from the international community, particularly the US, to enter into talks with Pakistan on the substantive issues related to Jammu & Kashmir. Secondly, India should expect not a diminishing but an increase in violent subversive activities by Pakistan not only in Jammu & Kashmir, but also in other parts of India. These anticipations are not speculative. Nawaz Sharif, in all his public pronouncements on the issue, has called for an immediate resumption of dialogue at the highest political level. India must also note the significant statement he made on 12 July 1999 in the Pakistan National Assembly that "though the volcanic eruption in Kargil has been brought under control, if India does not discuss Kashmir in a meaningful manner (meaningful means 'responsive to Pakistani demands'), other volcanoes will erupt." This pronouncement has to be noted with his earlier statement that there can be many more Kargils if India does not come to terms with Pakistan on Kashmir. The spokesman of the ISI, Brigadier Qureshi, when asked whether the so-called mujahideen were withdrawing, gave the ambiguous response, "I do not know. We have appealed to them. Maybe they are dispersing towards Srinagar."

Though India may legitimately feel a sense of relief that the Kargil conflict has come to an end, this should be tempered with a consciousness that the prospects of Indo-Pak relations remain uncertain and are fraught with possibilities of continuous covert subversion against India. The military and political leadership of Pakistan is projecting the Kargil episode as a "victory" on the following grounds: that Pakistani troops and Pakistani-supported mujahideen have successfully confronted Indian military forces; that Pakistan withdrew voluntarily for the cause of peace; that Pakistan achieved its chief political objective through reactivating international attention on the Kashmir issue, with the US pledging active interest by ensuring that a solution was Indo-Pak dialogue. Nawaz Sharif cannot but indulge in this kind of projection, given the failure of his government's misadventure.

What then are the lessons which we learn from this traumatic experience?

— Pakistan is not likely to agree to any practical solution of the Jammu & Kashmir issue on the basis of ground realities and reasonableness in the foreseeable future. It will continue its political campaign and overt military and terrorist operations against India, particularly in Jammu & Kashmir.
— Bilateral dialogue at the official and even at the highest political level with Pakistan should not be undertaken with any sense of excessive expectations, nor should it be predicated on the sincerity of Pakistan. Pakistan participates in these dialogues only as a strategem to keep the Kashmir issue alive and to

A Defining Moment

indulge in diplomacy and publicity to question the credibility and sincerity of purpose of India.

— Pakistan's unalterable objective is to capture Jammu & Kashmir. The substance of its India policy is related to this objective. The other diplomatic, political and publicity moves are calculated diversionary efforts.

— Pakistan will continue to foment military tension on the LoC and will indulge in intrusions to capture territory in Jammu & Kashmir. Pakistan will also engineer violence and terrorism in other parts of India in support of its proxy war in Kashmir. India should remain politically sensitive to these prospects at the policy level and should maintain continuous military alertness vis-á-vis Pakistan along the LoC as well as the international border. India will have to locate troops and security forces to the maximum extent possible on the LoC around the year. This has to be backed up by equipping our armed forces and updating our technological capacities to monitor and counter Pakistani military and other subversive moves. All this naturally would involve a substantial enhancement of financial resources for the armed forces. India has to monitor patterns of Pakistan's defence cooperation arrangements and defence procurement activities in foreign countries on a continuous basis, because that would enable it to anticipate future military operations by Pakistan.

— India should undertake a thorough overhauling of its intelligence gathering and intelligence assessment institutions and procedures both in functional and organisational terms. The interface between the intelligence agencies, the National Security Council and its adjuncts and the Cabinet Committee on Security Affairs has to be so organised that it does not face

surprise as well as confusion in command and control which it faced during the initial period of the Kargil conflict.
— Firmness in dealing with Pakistan at the operational plane combined with restraint gets India international support. We should nurture this policy stance.
— The support which India got on the Kargil conflict from the international community was Kargil-specific. There is no such support for India's overall stand on the Kashmir issue. The international community is keen that India and Pakistan quickly resolve this issue which, in their judgement, has the seeds of a nuclear and missile confrontation.
— India must also acknowledge that a solution to the Kashmir dispute has the imperative requirement of being responsive to the desires of the people of Jammu & Kashmir.
— International support for India's general concerns about its territorial integrity will depend on its appearing to be reasonable and willing to have a substantive dialogue with Pakistan on the issue of Jammu & Kashmir. A static stance by India will result in Pakistan regaining international support on the Kashmir issue.
— It is equally true that the international community does not support Pakistan's total claims on Jammu & Kashmir.
— Important powers are now inclined to a settlement of the Kashmir dispute with some kind of a Line of Control plus a package deal for autonomy for the people of Jammu & Kashmir with the added proviso for normal and free interaction between people living in Indian and Pakistan-held parts of Jammu & Kashmir. While India should be willing to resume dialogue with Pakistan, it must be clear in its mind that coming to a solution would be a gradual process spread over a decade or two. It must not let down its guard in any manner till then.

— A very important lesson to be kept in mind is the development of a US-China strategic consultation mechanism to deal with stability and security in a nuclear weaponised South Asian region. There is confirmed information that President Clinton and President Jiang Zemin were in more or less continuous contact during the period May to August 1999 on the Kargil conflict. US and Chinese policies on the subcontinental situation were coordinated at the highest level. India should be alert about the strategic implications of this development. Two superpowers having a converging approach on India's security environment can impact on our freedom of options.

In conclusion, one comes to the assessment that Pakistan cannot be trusted to come back to the negotiating table with any sincerity of purpose. However, Pakistan cannot avoid coming to the negotiating table due to considerations of *realpolitik* and requirements of international credibility. At the same time, Pakistan will continue its parallel diplomacy and proxy wars. The only way for India to deal with it is to be decisive and firm in its counter-measures. The objective should be to exhaust Pakistan and convince it that its military/terrorist misadventures will not be allowed to succeed.

Indo-Pak relations will remain tense for a decade or two unless something very drastic and miraculous happens, compelling Pakistan to come to a reasonable compromise and to have a normal working relationship with India. India must nevertheless continue its dialogue with Pakistan.

WINNING A REPRIEVE

■ SUNANDA K. DATTA-RAY

> Washington's facilitation in solving the Kargil crisis confirmed that an American stake in India's political integrity and economic prosperity would be a powerful defence against all forms of aggression, says the former editor of *The Statesman*.

The battle for Kargil did not win the war in Kashmir. Against External Affairs Minister Jaswant Singh's claim of "both a military and a diplomatic success" must be set the sombre warning by London's *Financial Times*: "One diplomatic triumph is not enough to change world opinion on Kashmir for ever and the tables could easily be turned." But the willingness this time of the Western allies (and perhaps even of China) to listen and respond to what India had to say demonstrated the truth of Lord Palmerston's famous dictum that nations have no eternal allies or perpetual enemies, but their interests are eternal and perpetual and they have a duty to follow them. This could mean a breakthrough in the process of building bridges with the United States that P.V. Narasimha Rao and Manmohan Singh initiated in the early nineties when India also began to cast aside the deadweight of patrician disapproval of all things American that swamped Jawaharlal Nehru's thinking.

Warts and all, the US is the only superpower we have. It sets the global compass. Waging a deadly battle against enemies within and without, India cannot do without it. South Asia is not normally high on their agenda. There were distractions enough in Kosovo, Northern Ireland and East Timor where the Western powers are more directly involved. But the end of the Cold War, the confusion in Russia, strains in Sino-American relations and the influence of domestic business lobbies had already prompted a policy reappraisal in Washington. Kargil indicated that the Americans, too, are seeking to improve ties with a stable, democratic and potentially dynamic nation of more than a billion people that might boast one of the world's biggest consumer markets. Moreover, a possible full-scale war between two nuclear weapon states could not be ignored.

Jaswant Singh's indefatigable diplomacy or the goodwill generated by President K.R. Narayanan's September 1998 tour of

Germany, Luxembourg and Portugal may not have been as productive without these factors. Pakistani Foreign Minister Sartaj Aziz may have helped to tilt the balance with his laughable contention that "no one knows where they (the invaders who had crossed the LoC in Kashmir) come from and who they are." Certainly, President Bill Clinton's ten-minute call to Prime Minister Atal Behari Vajpayee during a break in the Blair House tête-á-tête with Prime Minister Nawaz Sharif demonstrated an unusual consideration reflecting the changing US perception of India. So did the agreement on a Sino-Indian "security dialogue mechanism" reached during Jaswant Singh's trip to Beijing, the first exchange at this level in eight years.

This was *realpolitik*, pragmatism divorced from, though not necessarily devoid of, principle. The first lesson for New Delhi was that while it cannot disregard the geopolitical challenge of a highly volatile neighbour, it is essential to engage the principals who provide Islamabad with moral and material succour. The second was that it still has a long way to go in winning over the US. In spite of blaming Pakistan for the invasion and insisting that all the invaders pulled back ("We want to see the withdrawal of forces supported by Pakistan from the Indian side of the LoC," said James Rubin, the American state department spokesman), Washington was anxious that Sharif did not lose face. The Western media did not give him anything like the rough treatment that it meted out to Serbia's Slobodan Milosevic. Nor, in spite of speculation, did Clinton try to coerce the International Monetary Fund to withhold the next hundred million dollar instalment of a loan that the Pakistanis need desperately.

This concern can be rationalised as part of a desire to protect the fledgling confidence-building measures that Sharif and Vajpayee endorsed in February. The West may also hope that a gentler approach could still persuade Islamabad to sign the Comprehensive Test Ban Treaty. However, Washington's long-standing debt to Pakistan for services rendered during the Cold War, its determination to avoid what the Americans call a zero sum game in the subcontinent (meaning that relations with India will not be improved at the expense of relations with Pakistan), and lingering reservations about India also played a part in softening the blow.

Media coverage of the eleven weeks of bitter fighting with air and ground battles and more than twelve hundred casualties reflected this dichotomy. "Pakistan has been singled out by the West as the side which triggered the conflict," reported *The Financial Times* in tones of pained surprise. A long and graphic account in *Time* magazine described how soldiers of Pakistan's Northern Light Infantry Regiment and Khyber Rifles "discarded their uniforms for traditional salwar kameez or tracksuits, grew beards and wore traditional white religious skullcaps" to look like mujahideen before creeping over the thirty-five hundred metre high passes along the LoC to occupy the high ridges that the Indian Army had held in the summer. But most British and American publications also dwelt sympathetically on the problems Sharif was likely to face in getting the military and the mujahideen to pull back, and argued that converting the LoC into an international frontier — which India says it does not seek but might well find acceptable — would be an intolerable humiliation for Pakistan.

So far as Kashmir was concerned, Salman Rushdie's *New York Times* article, "Kashmir for the Kashmiris," a masterpiece of *suppressio veri, suggestio falsi*, put the heavily edited Pakistani-Western point of view succinctly. "Back in 1947 the state's Hindu maharaja 'opted' for India," he wrote, "and in spite of United Nations' resolutions supporting the largely Muslim population's right to a plebiscite, India's leaders have always rejected the idea, repeating over and over that Kashmir is 'an integral part' of India." Rushdie added in parenthesis, as if this explained the perfidy of "Hindu India," that "the Nehru-Gandhi dynasty is itself of Kashmiri origin."

Western reporters notoriously neglect their homework, especially when it comes to foreign, more particularly, Third World issues. In this instance, however, some of them turned out to be better informed (or more honest) than Rushdie. A few referred, albeit obliquely, to the 1947 invasion of Kashmir by hordes of tribesmen who had been armed and trained by the Pakistani Army and who subjected a defenceless populace to the horrors of murder, arson, loot and rape. One or two even hinted in passing at the Pakistani Army's participation in the attack. But constant harping on the Hindu maharaja and Muslim majority ignored the Buddhists of Ladakh and the Hindus of Jammu, making it look as if joining India was just a royal whim. No account recalled that Kashmir's legislature and Muslim prime minister ratified the act of accession — a gratuitous exercise in democratic and communal propriety that was not expected in any other princely state. No one thought it fit to identify the prime minister as the formidable Sheikh Mohammed Abdullah, whom his people called Sher-i-Kashmir (Lion of Kashmir), and who was at loggerheads with Maharaja Hari Singh.

The media sometimes tied itself up in knots trying to come to grips with this wealth of unfamiliar detail and nuances that blurred the approved pattern. It blamed Pakistan for the intrusion but credited it with a brilliant military victory for taking the heights and surprising the Indians in spite of the latter's superior military might. Supposedly straight news reports both praised India's "commendable restraint" in not crossing the LoC and lectured it for escalating the conflict, especially when Indian MiG-21s shot down a French-built Pakistani Atlantique-1 naval surveillance aircraft, killing all sixteen on board, in the Rann of Kutch, which is the only area outside Jammu & Kashmir that both countries claim. Not surprisingly, media indignation on that occasion reflected the views of the state department's Rubin who held that the border where the Atlantique intruded into India was "highly disputed". Indeed, media confusion conveyed something of the difficulty experienced by Western chancelleries on supporting India on Kargil without withdrawing support from Pakistan on Kashmir.

Indian ham-handedness in making tall or absurd claims came in for understandable criticism, though less often than in previous encounters. *The Economist* spotted the paradox of hostilities continuing unabated even though India claimed that its army had killed "almost as many (men) as it had said had invaded in the first place." London's *Independent* newspaper ridiculed a Bharatiya Janata Party spokesman who had confided in the British Broadcasting Corporation's *Today* programme that the Americans were fomenting conflict to control the Himalayas, the aim being "to keep an eye on India" from those lofty heights and to secure "a nice place for rest and recreation for American soldiers." All publications, including *The New York Times*, *The Washington Post* and *The Wall Street Journal* and, across the Atlantic, papers like London's *The Times, The Guardian, The Financial Times* and *The Independent* returned again and again to the original sin of Muslim Kashmir's allegedly forcible incorporation in "Hindu India" compounded by military repression, human rights abuses, three subcontinental wars and the refusal to hold a plebiscite.

Also taking their cue from authority, leading articles in serious American and British publications blew up the threat of nuclear war. Concern might have been justified to some extent since the effects of such a conflagration would obviously not be confined to the two contestants or even to the subcontinent. But neither the media nor governments took any notice of India's repeated assurances that it would not dream of using its nuclear weapons. India's belief that Pakistan was also responsible enough to exercise similar restraint cut no ice either. Instead, the West preferred to accept what the Pakistanis themselves chose to project, and which Ashley Tellis of the Rand Corporation described as "a classic form of nuclear coercion," Sharif called Kashmir "a nuclear flashpoint" and Benazir Bhutto spoke excitedly of an imminent "South Asian armageddon." Little wonder that *The New York Times* editorialised solemnly that "there is no guarantee that the presence of nuclear weapons on both sides will produce the kind of relatively stable balance of terror that prevailed between the US and the Soviet Union during the Cold War." In short, Asians cannot be trusted as Europeans can.

The Rushdie version, which is what Pakistan propagated and the West swallowed hook, line and sinker, also ignored the reason for United Nations' involvement. The world body did not become seized of the dispute because of any concern for suffering Muslims but because Nehru complained to it of Pakistan's military attack after Kashmir had acceded to India. He did, indeed, agree to hold a referendum but only in terms of the relevant United Nations resolutions that specified that this should be after troops had been pulled out. Since Kashmir was already juridically part of India, that meant that the Pakistanis would first have to relinquish control of the five thousand square miles they had overrun, the so-called "Azaad Kashmir."

Another factor that Western opinion, official and public, ignored is not part of the catechism of accession but deserves acknowledgement nonetheless. More than a hundred million Muslims would not still be living in India today if the two-nation theory advanced by Pakistan's founder, Mohammed Ali Jinnah, really had been the ultimate truth. They would have migrated en bloc to Pakistan like the exchange of population between Greece and Turkey under the 1923 Treaty of Lausanne. The emergence of Muslim Bangladesh, and the plight of fifty million Mohajirs (as immigrants from India are called) in Pakistan, further destroyed Pakistani pretensions to providing the subcontinent's Muslims with their only and legitimate sanctuary. In contrast, multi-religious and multi-ethnic India values Muslim and Buddhist Kashmiris as powerful ballast for its liberal secular cosmopolitanism.

Nevertheless, India and its friends took an exuberant view of the international response. Marika Vicziany, director of the Australian National Centre for South Asian Studies, went over the top to enthuse that "Pakistan has lost any past edge that it has over Kashmir." She may have erred on the side of understatement in claiming that "on many occasions, historically, the US has favoured Pakistan," but her conclusion that "the US ha(d) tilted towards India" applied only to the independently-corroborated cause of a localised conflict. If Pakistanis were as gloomy as Indians were jubilant, it was because they, too, are unaccustomed to American objectivity on this issue. Receiving no support for once, a Pakistani newspaper, *The Frontier Post*, accused the US and others of taking a "highly partisan and motivated approach to put Pakistan in the dock." The Clinton-Sharif statement was seen as a betrayal. Khalid Qayyum, chief reporter of another Pakistani newspaper, *The Nation*, summed it up in a front-page analysis: "The compromise on Kargil inked in Washington is being seen as Pakistan's worst-ever defeat on the diplomatic, political and media fronts."

The truth must lie somewhere between these extremes. Pakistan's hope, as the *Post* also admitted, was that the "Kargil imbroglio would awaken the international community to the Kashmir dispute's combustibility and stir it to action to defuse it once and for all." In this, the Pakistanis need not feel too disappointed. Sharif was not merely indulging in face-saving hyperbole when he broadcast that the withdrawal could take place since the objective of putting the status of Kashmir back on the international agenda had been achieved. Not all Indians agreed with the distinction Jaswant Singh drew between "internationalising" and "international concern." Kanti Bajpai, professor of strategic affairs at India's Jawaharlal Nehru University, for instance, argued that the Pakistanis had achieved some of their aims. "They have brought Kashmir back on the international map by reminding everyone that there is a problem here." According to Bajpai, the dispute "had been dead for two years" until the invasion and repulsion resuscitated it.

True, there was no mediation in the orthodox sense. Nothing came of media's suggestions that a role awaited China or the European Union. Or of Sharif's attempts to involve Kofi Annan, the United Nations secretary-general, appeals by Pakistan's Foreign Secretary, Shamshad Ahmad, to Western diplomats in Islamabad to send monitors to Kashmir and beef up the United Nations Military Observer Group which has about thirty personnel watching the LoC, or of Pakistan's complaint to the Security Council. The European Union Presidency advised India and Pakistan to act in accordance with existing undertakings and commitments, and the Group of Eight, which upheld the LoC and called for a resumption of the bilateral dialogue, condemned "military action to change the status quo" as "irresponsible." Neither was quite as forthright as the Americans or British prime minister Tony Blair who praised India's measured response to provocation, but no one supported direct third party intervention. Once bitten twice shy, even British Foreign Secretary Robin Cook made it clear that he was not offering to mediate.

Though the Americans claim to have defused a subcontinental war in 1990, Clinton was sufficiently sensitive to Indian susceptibilities not to try to emulate Harry S. Truman who angered Nehru by proposing Fleet Admiral Chester W. Nimitz, commander of the US Pacific Navy during Second World War, as Kashmir's plebiscite administrator. He did send envoys — General Anthony Zinni, the central command commander, to Islamabad and the state department's Gibson Lanpher to New Delhi — but, recognising that to play the mediator would be to side with Pakistan, the Fourth of July statement invoked the 1972 Simla accord. It also stressed the president's "personal interest" in encouraging bilateral efforts while Karl Inderfurth, the assistant under-secretary for South Asian affairs, found a word — "facilitation" — to describe Clinton's role without offending New Delhi.

India did not object since Sharif agreed in Washington to everything that India had been demanding — an end to the fighting and possible talks only after the occupying forces had retreated. But the Americans would certainly have been given a short and dusty answer if facilitation had condoned the Kargil intrusion or sought to settle the Kashmir question on Pakistan's terms. Pakistan's failure lay in not accomplishing what it had set out to do on the ground. It may have been masterly strategy to occupy the mountain peaks from which the Indian Army had withdrawn for the winter months. But India's vigorous rejoinder and concerted global pressure prevented the Pakistanis from entrenching themselves in their newly-gained positions, cutting off the Drass-Kargil highway, starving the Indian forces on the distant 6,600-metre-high Siachen glacier of supplies and creating the launching pad for a larger externally-inspired insurgency. "If you convince your people that you have got India by the jugular, and that there are going to be visible developments on Kashmir, then Pakistan has lost in terms of expectations raised," was the opinion of I.A. Rehman of the Human Rights Commission of Pakistan.

Western conditioning on Kashmir is attributable to two factors — the early success of Pakistani diplomacy and Cold War exigencies — that coalesced long before Pakistan turned itself into the base camp for the American-aided Afghan resistance against the Soviet occupation. Pakistan won the propaganda war then by convincing the United Nations General Assembly that Muslim-majority Kashmir could not possibly belong to "Hindu India." The argument was reinforced as India's political bungling compounded by its handling of the Pakistan-inspired terrorist campaign seemed to bear out the accusation that Kashmir was held by force. But this alone would not have had such a profound effect on American policy if Pakistan had not also made itself useful to the Western alliance.

The story is told of Winston Churchill, who had been invited to Buckingham Palace for lunch soon after India became a republic, booming from the drawing room threshold, "I believe I have the honour of being in the presence of Their Majesties the King and Queen of Pakistan!" His facetiousness masked a close cooperation that would not have been acceptable to Nehruvian India. It was the British who set the fashion that Henry Kissinger echoed many years later when he compared the "simpler, more direct" Pakistanis with their "intricate, complex" Indian neighbours, a comment that prompted the historians, Nathan and Sulochana Raghavan Glazer, to write: "If the representatives of India were more often generals, and the representatives of Pakistan were more often intellectuals and party politicians, conceivably we would be reading about 'intricate, complex Muslims' and 'simpler, more direct Hindus'." Indeed, this may have been one of Jaswant Singh's winning points in eight rounds of talks with Strobe Talbot, the American deputy secretary of state, between the May 1998 Pokharan tests and the Kargil conflict. For though he did not stay long enough in the Indian Army to wear a general's stars, the aristocratic Rajput minister is a former cavalry officer.

The West's dalliance with Pakistan began in March 1949 — Washington did not then expect Chiang Kai-shek to flee the Chinese mainland — when the American joint chiefs of staff drew up a memorandum in the light of the perceived threat from the Soviet Union. They dismissed South Asia — with one exception — as a region of "negligible positive strategic importance." The exception was Pakistan. "From the military point of view, the countries of South Asia excepting Pakistan have, under present and prospective conditions, little value to the US," read the memorandum, going on to say that "the Karachi-Lahore area" had "become of strategic importance" and "might be required as a base for air operations against central USSR and as a staging area for forces engaged in the defence or recapture of Middle East oil areas."

A month later the state department and army, navy and air force coordinating committee recommended "commercial arrangements which would in emergency facilitate development for operational use of base facilities in the Karachi-Lahore area." The report also pointed out that "so long as the defence of the Afghan frontier remains secure to us the air bases at Karachi,

Lahore, Rawalpindi and Peshawar might prove equally important in conducting air operations against the industrial areas of the Soviet heartland, or in defending Middle East oil." Moreover, Gordon P. Merriam of the policy planning staff, who was asked to explore the proposal for a Middle East defence arrangement (later the Baghdad Pact), reported that India's inclusion would make the group too large and unwieldy.

Neither the US nor Pakistan looked back after that. The nexus was most glaring in the previous round of subcontinental hostilities — the brief but bloody 1971 war — when India believed it was fighting for the humanitarian purpose of liberating Bangladesh from atrocities that were matched only by Cambodia's egregious Pol Pot regime. Yet, India's solitary supporter then was the small landlocked kingdom of Bhutan which had every geopolitical reason not to go counter to the wishes of Pakistan's staunch ally and sponsor, China, and yet did so.

Just as no one was willing to see India as the victim of aggression in 1947, no one saw India as the victim in 1965 when Field Marshal Ayub Khan's Operation Malta repeated that invasion with his five-thousand-man Gibraltar Force, setting another precedent for Kargil. The 1962 border war with China was about the only conflict in which India was not thoroughly isolated. Most Asian governments sat on the fence even then, urging New Delhi to come to terms with Beijing. The Americans, who had not yet found in the Chinese either a valuable ally against Moscow's "evil empire" or a market promising handsome returns, were markedly more sympathetic. But even they could not help gloating. John F. Kennedy told India's ambassador, Braj Kumar Nehru, that India had been hoist with its own petard — or, as he put it more colourfully, the world was clapping because the preacher had been caught in a brothel, and he was clapping too.

Preachy or not, India could not convince others of the legitimacy of its actions in respect of the princely states of Hyderabad and Junagadh, the Portuguese colony of Goa and the protected kingdom of Sikkim. Memory is never allowed to die. Even when Kargil was being discussed in the British House of Commons, Lorna Fitzsimons, the Labour MP for the Lancashire town of Rochdale, brought up Hyderabad and Junagadh, apologising for her "northern" pronunciation of the latter as "Juna Garh." Of course, not every incorporation of territory was morally or legally justifiable; but the world's reaction was uniformly censorious. Kissinger's description of Indira Gandhi as "a cold-blooded practitioner of power politics" summed up what the West thought (or affected to think) of the pious rhetoric in which Indian leaders habitually clothed whatever they did.

At the start, the West greeted India with a burst of euphoric acclaim, Dean Acheson writing, a la Voltaire's comment on God, that Nehru was so important to mankind that he would have had to be invented if he had not already existed. But it soon became fashionable to be dismissive of the subcontinent and its quarrels. Traces of that attitude surfaced during the Kargil crisis in a *Wall Street Journal* leader that described India and Pakistan as "dangerous pests on the world stage" who seemed "incapable of exterminating the threat that their enmity poses" to others. An Australian diplomat told me that the organisers of international conferences found it tiresome having to set aside the first half-an-hour for, as he put it, "the Indians and the Pakistanis to have a go at each other." Some global leaders must have shared the nonchalance of Jeremy Thorpe, the last of Britain's grand Liberal politicians, who likened Kashmir to the Schleswig-Holstein dispute which, said Lord Palmerston, only three people ever understood — the Prince Consort who was dead, a Danish politician who was mad, and he himself and he had long ago forgotten all about it. But the sophisticated Thorpe was not obliged to take sides. Those who were knew their geostrategic onions — a staunch member of the Regional Cooperation for Development (the alliance of Pakistan, Turkey and the Shah's Iran which grew out of the Baghdad Pact) was any day preferable to a leading and highly articulate nonaligned nation, even if it was the world's biggest democracy.

Things began to change only when the Soviet Union's disintegration made it unnecessary to post a gendarme in Southwest Asia. Washington had previously ignored American Central Intelligence Agency reports on Chinese and North Korean collusion over Pakistan's nuclear and missile programmes or about Pakistani exports of arms and spares to Middle East destinations. The allegations came under closer scrutiny as the winds of Islamic fundamentalism swept the globe. To the nightmare of an Islamic Bomb, the spectre of Osama Bin Laden, the renegade Saudi Arabian billionaire, and worries about Iraq, Afghanistan and Libya was added the more troubling question of what oil-rich Saudi Arabia might be up to. The Americans complained of a lack of clarity when the Saudi defence minister, Prince Sultan Bin Abdelaziz al-Saud, the king's powerful brother, visited Pakistan in May and toured its missile and nuclear facilities. It was a "definitely eyebrow-arching" event for the US, where a military spokesman added that Riyadh had "obfuscated" the event. "The Saudis haven't told us the purpose of the visits and the Pakistanis have discounted them."

Slow in coming, this cooling-off may also have coincided with a reappraisal in Beijing. Though China joined the US to inveigl against South Asian nuclear developments, singling out India for harsh condemnation, Chinese and American interests in Asia have diverged, at least for the time being. China's shrill opposition to the Kosovo bombing was followed by the official *China Daily* cautioning Pakistan against encouraging or even risking Western involvement in Kashmir. There is no reason to suppose that the Sino-Pakistan entente has been weakened — Pakistan's army chief, General Parvez Musharraf, was in Beijing when the shooting started and Sharif and his foreign minister both followed him there — but the Chinese do not want Kashmir or Kosovo to set a precedent for Tibet and Xinjiang, especially with reports of Pakistan-trained Muslims in the latter province. And the deadlock with the US over Taiwan, East Asia's proposed theatre missile defence system to create a protective shield for Japan, South Korea and possibly Taiwan, political slush funds and nuclear espionage may have strengthened the resolve to close ranks in Asia.

Hence China's "studiously neutral" statements, to cite *The Economist*, that "said nothing about an immediate cease-fire which would leave Pakistani forces on Indian territory" and refusal to "link withdrawal (from Kargil) to a solution of the wider Kashmir issue." This coolness must disturb the Pakistanis more than even Washington's stand. Writing to a London-based Pakistani publication, *The News International*, Azmat A. Khan, secretary-general of the Jammu & Kashmir Liberation Front's United Kingdom-Europe branch, voiced the fear that there had already been "a notable shift" towards India in China's "allegiance." He did not discount the possibility that in the pursuit of a regional role for itself, China might emerge as the new mediator in South Asia.

India and Pakistan must both look within for answers. For an economically vibrant and politically confident India, a return to the time "when even Kashmiri Muslims thought secular India would protect their distinct identity better than avowedly Islamic Pakistan" (*The Economist*) would remove or, at least, reduce the scope for external mischief. Even *The Economist* believes "that trust could be revived." Satisfying legitimate Kashmiri aspirations within the national framework should not be an impossible objective for a country whose strength lies in its diversity and which has subsumed the Tamil (the old Dravida Munnetra Kazagham), Naga, Mizo, Khalistan and other secessionist movements.

"We want a modern, close and forward-looking partnership," Geoffery Hoon, Britain's minister of state in the foreign and commonwealth office, said of India in the Commons. So do the Americans, whose policy planners at the Pacific Command headquarters in Honolulu describe India as one of the centres that will project economic and political power — military power follows — in a multipolar twenty-first century. In spite of ups and downs, Indians have less reason now to complain of the mix of benign neglect and malign interest that was said to constitute American diplomacy right up to the time when Narasimha Rao and Manmohan Singh changed India's course in a dramatic revolution whose impact has not yet been felt fully. A resolution of the impasse with Pakistan would obviously further strengthen ties. Conversely, only a firm partnership with the US would serve notice on Pakistani militarists not to indulge in more gambles like the Kargil adventure. It is the old chicken-and-egg situation in which India's, as well as the subcontinent's, welfare is hostage to Kashmir, and, therefore, also to Washington's perception of its strategic interests in the region.

India is on trial. It has won a reprieve from the usual international censure. But electoral uncertainty, a retreat to autarky or nuclear irresponsibility could easily dissipate the advantage it now enjoys. So might an escalation of the Kashmir rebellion, especially now that Indonesia has succumbed to Western pressure over East Timor. On the other hand, Washington's facilitation in solving the Kargil crisis confirmed that an American stake in India's political integrity and economic prosperity would be a powerful defence against all forms of aggression, overt and insidious, as well as against the sabotage and subversion that are increasingly the supplementary weapons of subcontinental warfare. It would mean stepping up economic reforms instead of military spending, opening markets rather than closing borders, and restoring the flagging promise of liberalisation. The answers to India's external problems are all to be found at home.

A Fatal Love

■ Suketu Mehta

> The men who killed each other in Kargil were dealing with the unfinished business of Partition, argues the writer, who believes that the people of the two countries have a fatal love for each other.

A Fatal Love

To understand what happened in Kargil you have to go back half a century, to the colossal and premature sundering of the subcontinent known as Partition. The men who killed each other over Tiger Hill and Drass and Batalik were dealing with the unfinished business of Partition. I have no personal experience of Partition; my family is Gujarati, from Calcutta and Kenya, and I have no relatives in Pakistan or Bangladesh. My own partition was at the age of fourteen, when I immigrated with my family to New York. I am a novelist. What I try to do is to get to the struggling human being underneath the massive foot of history. The greatest scholar of Partition was a fiction writer, Saadat Hasan Manto, a man who died in Lahore mourning his separation from a whore named Bombay. "Uper di gur gur di mung dal...", chants the madman in "Toba Tek Singh." Fiction writers and lunatics have their own truth. Our enemies are the writers of school textbooks. As the Czech poet Jaroslav Seifert said: for anybody else, not to tell the truth can be a tactical manoeuvre. But a writer who is not telling the truth — is lying.

My family borders are not subcontinental; they are international. But Partition, like the Big Bang, has echoes that will forever permeate the universe of people I write about. In my work, in my fiction as well as in my nonfiction, I have been looking at riots, at communal conflict, in Banaras, Punjab, and especially Mumbai. Most of this conflict has its roots in Partition — "batwara," which in different circumstances could also have meant "sharing." It is a family quarrel, as when three brothers live side by side in the same house, walling up the rooms, always conscious of the others in the rooms beyond. Kargil is only the latest battle in that endless property dispute; the brothers have come to blows in the street. There will be more to come, before the children grow up and say to their fathers and uncles: Enough.

There are millions of Partition stories throughout the subcontinent, a body of lore that is infrequently recorded in print or on tape, and rarely passed on to the next generation. All over the map of South Asia, there is an entire generation of people who have been made poets, philosophers, and storytellers by their experiences during Partition. Any person over fifty-five or sixty in Delhi or Amritsar or Lahore has stories to tell of that period, even if they were not themselves dislocated then. And for those who have been displaced from their birthplaces against their will and at an early age, the impression of home is all the more vivid and sharp; it haunts their dream-lives, and their minds are the battleground between the desire to forget and the need to remember.

In the summer of '97, I travelled to the Wagah border, and then on to Lahore. It was through Wagah and the nearby town of Attari that most of the Punjabi refugees came through, crossing east to India or west to Pakistan. It was here, in a dingy tourist hotel room on the border, that two seventy-year-old Sikh men, Santokh Singh and Harjeet Singh, told me what they did one afternoon fifty years ago, when their minds went mad.

One day in August 1947, Santokh Singh said, an old Sikh man in a village near Attari, out on a walk to buy milk, was murdered by some Muslims. Santokh Singh was a student then, a "leader-type," as he refers to himself. Ten Sikh men gathered to take revenge. Before they went on their expedition, they went to the gurdwara and took an oath not to kill or molest women and children. Then Santokh Singh put on his armoured vest. He took a revolver. They went to the Muslim part of the village. One member of their band grabbed a Muslim woman, but he was reminded of his oath by the others.

Santokh Singh did not tell me what happened next. "My mind

went mad for one day," is all he would say. "We took revenge here, they took revenge there," he shrugged. He did not seem to be much affected now by whatever he did then. But on the day after they took their revenge, Santokh Singh's father asked him why he, a strapping twenty-one-year-old man, looked so sad. He had been watching the Muslim women and children going over the border, people he had grown up with. "Mere jigar ke tukde jaa rahe hain," he said. "Parts of my heart are going across."

The next morning, he brought along a friend. Harjeet Singh was another of that band of ten men. He looked at a map in the lobby of the hotel. It was a large map of undivided Punjab, Maharaja Ranjit Singh's Punjab. "Even now the heart...," he started saying, and his eyes reddened, his voice thickened. He was a thin, dignified man who has done well with his wheat and rice farms. He has a daughter in the US, and a son in Toronto, and has travelled there, marvelling at the friendship between Canada and the US, the free trade over the border.

Harjeet Singh repeated, as a prelude, what Santokh Singh had stressed. "When the old man was killed, nobody could hold back. But we didn't touch any woman or child."

"There was much junoon (madness). It lasted fifteen to twenty days. When we heard that injured bodies, dead bodies were coming in the trains people were going crazy. Then when the old man was killed, nobody could hold back." They got guns, swords, spears, scythes. Then they went to the Muslim village. "It lasted just a few hours. At most two people killed the old man, so we should only have looked for them." Harjeet Singh knew some of the people in the village — they were his classmates. He was looking out for them, to save them, but they were not there. The Sikhs rounded up the Muslim men, and gathered the women and children to one side. "We killed one third of the people in that village. About fifty to sixty men were killed in those few hours. The women and children were put to one side but they were watching; they were screaming. In some places there was fighting, but they weren't begging for mercy — by that time everyone knew that asking for mercy was meaningless, there wasn't much being said."

Harjeet Singh was weeping profusely by now, his handkerchief going now to one eye, now to the other. It was obvious that he was saying some things for the first time; at this point, he was not even talking directly to me. Every journalist knows that this is when the really important stories come out, when the person you're interviewing stops talking to you, and is really explaining things to himself. "I don't get angry on anybody else but myself. I didn't sleep all that night, I didn't stop thinking about it for a single minute. That's the worst memory for me."

What happened to the survivors, I asked him.

"Then they walked to Pakistan. I've never met any one of them after that — not even my classmates, the ones who got saved."

How does a man live with having murdered his neighbours? Harjeet Singh's way of atonement has been through a constant searching out of the Other, a series of highly emotional meetings with his former enemies. He has crossed the border no fewer than three times since then, a feat whose magnitude can be appreciated by any Indian trying to get a visa at the Pakistani embassy in Delhi. On his trips, he tries to meet his former neighbours, the Muslims from Attari whom he had a hand in driving out.

The first time Harjeet Singh went to Pakistan was 1956, and he went with his wife. An entire convoy of vehicles came to the border to receive the Attari group, twenty-five to thirty trucks, five to seven buses, cars. They were the Muslims who had been driven out. The group from Attari had to stay at each of their houses in turn, and nobody took money for lunch or dinner, or

A Fatal Love

for petrol. But on the 1956 trip, he says, "The younger generation looked at us with a certain amount of hatred."

Harjeet Singh's wife's village was in Pakistan. When they went back, he said, "They knew I was the son-in-law of the family; they just held me and burst out crying." He met the people who had worked in the household of his wife's family. "Whatever money they had, they just emptied their pockets and gave me." He was, after all, the returning son-in-law. After all these years, he says, "my wife was still a daughter of the village."

In 1980, one of Harjeet Singh's cousins went to Pakistan, and Harjeet asked him to look up his best friend before Partition, a Muslim who was so close to him that he would eat a chicken that Harjeet had cooked, even if it was not halal. The Muslim friend received the cousin with great hospitality, and then asked him a favour. Would he bring Harjeet Singh to the border? He wanted to meet him, just once.

The cousin went back to Attari and passed on the message. Harjeet Singh went to the border at the appointed time. "All the security men said, you must be mad. You can't meet." Across the fence, Harjeet Singh, after thirty-three years, saw his friend, who rushed forward, only to be pushed back by the Pakistani security men far beyond the fence. Harjeet saw that his friend was straining against them, weeping. At first Harjeet turned back, but a relative who knew the soldiers intervened on his behalf. The Indian major talked to his Pakistani counterpart. So Harjeet Singh went forward with two of his youngest children beyond the fence and his friend came forward to meet him. They embraced each other; they were overwhelmed and there was no point in talking. What could be said? How does one condense the highlights of three decades? His friend was crying, but Harjeet Singh was determined not to. Harjeet Singh apologised — for not having brought all of his children to show his friend. "I said I'm sorry. My two girls are married in different villages; I didn't have time to get them all here to show you."

Then the soldiers separated the two men and his friend went back into Pakistan and Harjeet Singh started walking slowly back into India. He was stopped by agents from the Intelligence Bureau, and they asked him, "Who were you talking to?" "To my brother," Harjeet Singh answered. How can that be, they demanded, he was Sikh, the man who came to meet him was Muslim. "I said that's exactly what I mean, he's my brother. He has land on that side, I have land on this side, that's why we're separated." The Intelligence men said, "Don't fool us." I said, "I have told you what I told you, I have said what I have said, he is my brother."

Again, in 1982, Harjeet Singh crossed the border. He went with his daughter to a village on the other side where a group of Muslim brothers from Attari had settled. Some of them were wrestlers; they had gone there and become sweetsellers and made three good houses. But now there was only one of the brothers left. Harjeet Singh and his daughter went to the old man's house for dinner, and talked with the sweet-merchant's entire family late into the night about the village. If the border were opened up tomorrow, said the old man to Harjeet Singh, his children would drive there, because they had cars. "But," said the old man, "I'll still beat them because I'll run so fast." In the morning when they woke up the old man said, "I'm going to tell you something...," and then all his grandchildren rushed forward and interrupted him. "We're going to tell you what he was going to say. He'll say I had a dream last night that I was in Attari. Uncle, every morning when he wakes up he says he's met this person in Attari, that person in Attari." This was in

A Fatal Love

1982, thirty-five years after the old man had left his village. At least in his waking life.

It is a common desire among those displaced by Partition to make the return crossing, to try to go home again. The Pakistani writer Intizar Husain, whom I met in Lahore, told me that for thirty years he had tried to get a visa to go back to India, particularly to the village he was born in, Dibai, near Aligarh in Uttar Pradesh. Although he has been living in Lahore since 1947, most of his fiction is set in Dibai. Like the old sweetseller from Attari, he had also been having a recurring dream. "I go there, to my home, and am wandering among the houses. Those lanes, those palaces. The terraces where we flew kites," and then he described his house for me, constructing it lovingly in the air with his hands. "The Muslim quarter began at our house. The terraces of the Hindu houses were so close that at Diwali time I would reach across, steal oil lamps from their terraces, and bring them home."

Thirty years later, at the invitation of a literary gathering in Delhi, Husain was able to get a visa to go back. He was in Aligarh, and then made an impulsive decision to revisit Dibai, which his visa did not allow him to do. He persuaded an Indian friend to drive him to the village. On the way, he saw the trucks all along the road, the phantom convoys of Partition. As they came into the village, he couldn't believe how much it had changed. There used to be a pilgrim's hostel. Where was the hostel? Where was the hospital? Everything had become a bazaar. He looked for his house, but the geography of home had changed. His companion said, "Why don't you ask someone?" "I said I have come to my own town. I am not going to ask someone else for directions." Husain got out of the car and wandered the bazaars but could not locate his birthplace, and something in him would not let him ask a stranger for guidance in the territory of his own childhood, his own dreams. At last, he got back in the car, and drove back to Aligarh. He never found his childhood home. He has never gone back.

I asked Husain why there were no museums, no memorials to that time. He responded, "It is good that the killings are not memorialised, that there are no pictures of those times." I found this curious, coming from a writer whose entire body of work deals with "those times." What tormented him, he seemed to be saying, was his generation's burden alone. What use would it be to rake up the past, to keep harping on the atrocities of Partition? If the current generation could only forget what his generation went through, then maybe they could start talking to each other.

Beware of the past: turn back to look at it and the one you love will be cast into hell, like Eurydice, or you will be turned into a pillar of salt, like Lot's wife. The past is a dangerous place, for it is where home lies.

I respectfully differ with Intizar Husain. I think there should be museums, memorials, a supreme subcontinental storytelling. I think that recounting the atrocities of Partition might have the opposite effect from that feared by Husain: it will inoculate us against repeating them. It is interesting to compare the experiences of Holocaust survivors with Partition survivors. The world has come around to the notion that the great crime that happened in Europe in the forties is worthy of minute examination — a tidal wave of films, books, and television shows drive home the point, almost to exhaustion. But it barely has a notion of what was happening at the same time in South Asia. Among the Partition survivors, I have found surprisingly little bitterness against the perpetrators. Fifty years is a long time to live with trauma, and a great many of the survivors have found that the only way to maintain their mental balance is to forgive the aggressors. I was

A Fatal Love

struck by the fact that many of the people telling me their stories were telling them to someone outside the family for the very first time, and they were astonished that anybody would be interested.

The strongest need to tell is not that of the victims of violence; it is that of the perpetrators. What did we do to each other? Examine your hands: they are covered in blood long dried. Who made us do this? We can't just blame the conqueror. "I don't get angry on anybody else except myself," Harjeet Singh said to me in that hotel room in Wagah. It is an existential burden. Which one of us is capable of killing? What authority are we submitting to, whose orders do we obey when we kill?

Harjeet Singh did not explicitly say that he keeps travelling to Pakistan to atone for what he did. But when he told me his story, weeping, wailing, it was evident that it was in the nature of a confessional. In drawing out such narratives, I have found strong initial resistance; but once the telling begins, it is nearly impossible to stop it. It comes out in a flood. The perpetrators were not professional murderers or rapists. They were village folk, by and large. Farmers, grocers, neighbours. In Punjab they call it the "junoon". It was a period suspended in time, separate from what came before and what came after. It was a mad time, and madness is their excuse for what they did. "Uper di gur gur di mung dal...." They have lived the past fifty years with the moral responsibility for what they did. At an individual level, these human beings who murdered other human beings are perfect fictional characters. Fiction, as Faulkner said, is about the human heart in conflict with itself.

For fifty years the telling has stopped. A whole generation didn't want to talk about it to their sons and daughters; a whole generation didn't want to hear about it. The telling is for the grandchildren. Now there is a generation of grandchildren in all three countries that is coming to power, and they have the luxury of forgiving, a luxury their parents did not enjoy.

But there are two competing forces in the telling: the grandparents and the governments. The governments have their own ideas of the story, and they have the power of the state to spread their version, through textbooks. School textbooks on both sides, written as always by professional liars, gloss quickly over Partition, preferring to concentrate on the struggle for independence, a much more noble chapter in the subcontinent's history. When Partition is dealt with at all, it is portrayed as a massacre of our people by their people. The way we gained independence is something to be proud of, an example to other nations. What followed is our shared secret shame. But surely Partition, the splitting up of the subcontinent and the mass transfer of populations, was a far more important historical event than independence from a foreign power which ruled parts of the region for less than two hundred years, an eyeblink in South Asian history.

The history of Partition and the independence struggle, points out Husain, gets distorted in both countries. "I was seeing episodes of the freedom struggle on Indian television. I was surprised to see that Maulana Muhammad Ali, Shaukat Ali were completely absent. Jinnah also. Why had they disappeared?" The results of this willed amnesia are apparent in a poll of urban youth aged eighteen to twenty-five, commissioned in May 1997 by the newsmagazine *Outlook*. When asked which state was most affected by Partition, fifty-nine per cent said Kashmir; only thirty-nine per cent identified Punjab. When asked to identify places associated with Partition violence, the majority (fifty-three per cent) picked Jallianwala Bagh.

So the child growing up in Lahore or Delhi or Dhaka shuttles between two tellings: what he is instructed at school, which he will have to learn by rote and regurgitate in the examinations, and what his old grandmother tells him in the last room of the house about the days of the junoon.

Who is the telling directed towards? Why is it necessary? The new generation has no sense of Partition. We have grown up, and our parents have grown up, with the reality of three separate states and most of us are satisfied with the arrangement. We do not want to merge into one colossal super-state. I ask those who want to undo Partition: have we really managed India, Pakistan, and Bangladesh so well from Delhi, Islamabad, and Dhaka, that we want to push it still further to fold everything back into one? What is needed is far greater decentralisation, not the opposite. Perhaps a future in which the various states of the subcontinent split off into autonomous entities is not so bad, is inevitable and even desirable. Kashmir has as much right to self-government in local matters as does Karnataka or Karachi. What is possible is a common market, free movement of people across open borders, even a common currency. Everything else should be radically decentralised.

What still brings us together? Paan (betel-leaf) and music. On the Samjhauta Express between Delhi and Lahore I saw everybody carrying baskets of betel-leaf. It is among the biggest items of trade between the two countries; a South Asian bad habit. Through the three wars, through the problems over Kashmir, through cricket matches, through Thackeray and the Jamaat, people have needed to chew paan. India grows it; Pakistan chews it. People in Lahore will curse the Indian Army through a mouthful of paan grown in the enemy country. As for music, Bade Ghulam Ali Khan Saheb, who after 1947 shuttled restlessly back and forth between the two countries, unable to find home, put it best. He said, "If classical music had been taught in every home in India and Pakistan, there wouldn't have been a Partition."

The first time I met the enemy people, Pakistanis, was when I went to New York. We shopped together, we ate together, we dated each other and had each others' babies. A phenomenon I have been noticing lately is that of the young NRI student coming to Delhi for the Christmas holidays, and saving a week to go to Karachi or to Lahore, to attend the wedding of a college roommate. It is there, abroad, where exiles gather, that there are signs that Partition might not be irreversible. I used to shop at a store in Jackson Heights, Queens, advertising "Indo-Pak-Bangladeshi-Afghan Groceries." I know of a gang in the high schools of Flushing, comprising of juvenile delinquents of South Asian descent — Muslim, Sikh, Hindu kids fighting together, united against the Koreans, the Hispanics, the African-Americans. The cafeteria below where I used to work in Manhattan sold rice and dal to taxi drivers from all across the subcontinent; turbaned cabbies sporting Khalistani slogans on their cabs stood next to Punjabi Hindus with VHP stickers on theirs, and ate together and talked about the mustard fields of their villages. There are an astonishing number of Pakistanis dating Indians in Wembley and in Jackson Heights. It is almost as if the Enemy is deliberately sought out, wooed. These are by and large children of very conservative parents, who have raised them on a diet of patriotic hatred. So teenage rebellion travels hand in hand with repudiation of their parents' hatreds. The young people are determined to transgress the ultimate boundary with the Other, by accepting them into their bed.

Most progressive organisations in North America take pains to call themselves "South Asian," rather than Indian or Pakistani or Bangladeshi. It is always when the quarrelling family leaves its house that it comes back together again. These walls, these fences we have put up on our borders: they are of recent vintage, and they are flimsy. We have watered them with our blood, and they have come up weeds.

The massacres of Partition were the first act of a great love, an illicit love, worthy of a Sufi qawaali or a Bhakti bhajan or a Bollywood blockbuster. The three-and-a-half wars we have fought since then comprise the second act. We are nearing the last act, the logical and mythic end.

We the peoples of the subcontinent respect illicit love; we know that the most powerful love is the hidden love, the secret longing of the individual soul for an absent God. I have a Sindhi friend in Bombay whose father, a doctor, left Karachi only in 1965. Well after independence, he kept on his practice in Karachi. Among his clients were the women of a brothel. His wife always knew when he had treated one of them, because the notes he brought home that day would be scented. For some reason, the prostitutes preferred Hindu doctors — they thought the Hindus would not take liberties with them. They were also quite shy around the doctor; when he would go to examine them, they would unveil only the affected part; so he saw their bodies only in segments, never whole. One day one of the prostitutes, whom he had now known for a long time, asked him if he would come to her room. He wasn't sure what she wanted, and was hesitant, but she insisted. Come to my room, doctor, she said. And she led him inside when no-one was looking, and locked the door. Then she opened the almirah in the back of the room, and showed him her secret inside. He came closer, and saw what she was pointing at: it was a small shrine, with a statue of Lord Krishna. Lifting her veil, the prostitute told him that she prayed to Krishna every day. She was a Hindu woman who had been kidnapped during Partition, forced to convert, and then sold to this brothel. But she maintained, in the silences of her room, this illicit lover, Krishna, through all these long years. That was all the prostitute was asking of the doctor: to bear witness to her love, to the truth of her love.

Love can still be mythic in South Asia. There is a reason that South Asian writers are suddenly in vogue in the West. It is because we are a storehouse, a seed bank, of myth. Our leading exports are software, jewels, and myths. Is there any such thing as forbidden love in Paris, in New York? There, the greatest tragedy possible with love is that it can end in marriage and divorce; here, it could end in death.

I am thinking now about Kunwar Ahson and Riffat Afridi in Karachi. In Pakistan in 1998, a Pathan girl dared to love a Mohajir boy. It was because of Partition that the boy was born in Karachi, but there were other borders which could never be crossed. The girl's relatives, her tribe, went gunning for the boy; and they were prepared to kill their own daughter. The entire city went up in riots; two people were killed, dozens injured. The police arrested the boy and beat him badly in the prison. The girl was brought to court to repudiate her love; she came in her wedding dress. She addressed the judge from behind her veil; lifted her eyes and said her truth: that she loved Kunwar Ahson. She had taken him as her husband. The bloodthirsty mob bayed its sentence outside. When the boy appeared in court, the girl's relatives were waiting for him, with the compliance of the police. They riddled his body with bullets. Kunwar Ahson now lies in some hospital, paralysed for life, unable to consummate the love he nearly lost his life for (and this, too, fits within the story; for such a love should always be the love of angels, a chaste love, in which lust has no part). The girl is hidden with his parents, unable to meet her lover. Both of them are now begging the world to give them safe shelter somewhere else, for such love is dangerous in a region where love still has power.

I find their love important, metaphorical. Against great odds — against the tyrant father of the State — we the peoples of the subcontinent love each other. It is an adulterous love, an illicit love. When we want to live together safely, it has to be outside, in some other country, in someone else's house. It is still a land where love means something, because we are ready to die for love. We are ready to kill for love. Such is the strength of our passion for each other that we have no other way of proving this love than to die for it. Any lesser climax would be to mock the vastness, the wholeness, of this love; could it be tested, satiated, by mere exile or maiming? We are determined to die, for love; we have made a collective suicide pact. Each one of us will kill the other. We will show the whole world what love is; we will all go out in a grand gesture, all together at once, in the space of fifteen minutes. This can be the only fit ending to such a great love.

NOTES ON CONTRIBUTORS

RAHUL BEDI is the New Delhi-based correspondent for *The Daily Telegraph*, London and *Jane's Defence Weekly*, UK. He has reported extensively on security-related affairs from India and specialises in military matters.

BHARAT BHUSHAN is the executive editor of *The Hindustan Times*. Earlier, he was a special correspondent with *The Times of India* and then the Washington correspondent of *The Indian Express*.

PAMELA CONSTABLE is the New Delhi-based South Asia bureau chief for the *Washington Post*. Over her twenty-five year career, she has reported from more than twenty countries, including Chile, Haiti, Cuba Russia, South Korea, the Philippines and El Salvador. She has previously worked for the *Boston Globe* and the *Baltimore Sun*.

LT. GEN. MOTI DAR was the vice-chief of army staff in 1995-1996. He served in Kargil as brigade-major from 1967 to 1970, and has also commanded a brigade in Ladakh. He fought in both the 1965 and 1971 wars with Pakistan.

SAURABH DAS has been a photographer with the Associated Press since 1996; he was with *The Asian Age* earlier. His photographs were accepted in Joop Swart Masterclass of World Press, 1999.

SUNANDA K. DATTA-RAY is a regular columnist in *The International Herald Tribune* and *Time* magazine and has been editor of *The Statesman* (Calcutta and Delhi); editor-in-residence, the East-West Centre, Honolulu, Hawaii, USA; and editorial consultant, *The Straits Times*, Singapore.

J.N. DIXIT was India's foreign secretary from 1991 to 1994 and is currently a member of the National Security Advisory Board. He is a professor at the Centre for Policy Research, New Delhi, and has lectured widely in Indian and foreign universities.

Notes on Contributors

MUZAMIL JALEEL is the Srinagar-based senior correspondent of *The Indian Express*. He was awarded a fellowship by The Times of India group in 1994 to work on, "Implications of Violence on Kashmiri Society."

SUKETU MEHTA is at work on a non-fiction book on Mumbai and on a novel. He is a winner of the Whiting Writer's Award and the O'Henry Prize for short fiction. His short stories and articles have appeared in *Granta*, *Time* magazine, *Harper's* magazine and *Indian Literature*. His essay in this book was first delivered as a talk at the Centre for the Study of Developing Societies in New Delhi.

SANKARSHAN THAKUR is the New Delhi-based associate editor of *The Telegraph*. He began his journalistic career with *Sunday* magazine in 1984 and joined the Delhi bureau of *The Telegraph* in 1985.